Smarter Retirement Planning

A Practical Guide Inspired by How Advisors Plan

Alan M Fischer, RICP

ISBN: 979-8-9987260-1-9

A Word From Early Readers

"I've read a lot of financial books over the years, and most of them focus on investments, returns, or 'beating the market.' This one does something different—and more important. *Smarter Retirement Planning* doesn't try to turn you into a stock picker. It teaches you how to think.

Instead of chasing performance, it walks you through how advisors actually approach retirement: mapping income over time, understanding withdrawal sequencing, documenting investment decisions, and planning for risk before it shows up.

The tone is calm, practical, and grounded in real-world experience—not hype. No scare tactics. No magic formulas. Just clear thinking and actionable structure.

If you've saved well but want greater clarity about how your retirement plan works, this book will help you see your finances differently."

— Mike D., Business Owner & Author

This testimonial was given by a client of the financial advisor, and no compensation was provided directly or indirectly. This testimonial is not a guarantee of future performance or investment success, and the testimonial may not be representative of the experience of other customers. Please visit BrokerCheck (https://brokercheck.finra.org) to see more on the background of this professional.

This book is a **must** read if you are planning to navigate your retirement on your own. As for me, that is a path I would not consider taking --- however, this book is written in a way that even a novice can understand all of the pieces that need to be taken into consideration. It is likely that after reading this, you may have a change of heart and decide you would rather work with a financial advisor --- but now you will be armed with knowledge to have an educated conversation with them on the decisions being made.

— **Carol W – Business Leader**

This testimonial was given by a client of the financial advisor, and no compensation was provided directly or indirectly. This testimonial is not a guarantee of future performance or investment success, and the testimonial may not be representative of the experience of other customers. Please visit BrokerCheck (https://brokercheck.finra.org) to see more on the background of this professional.

Alan Is the real deal. He lives a guided life with purpose enjoying the freedom that his career has allowed him to achieve. He challenges people's assumptions about their current situation and the potential retirement to give them the freedom that he enjoys in his own life. He's an advocate for the people in his life whether they are clients, acquaintances, or other business professionals he networks with. He gives more than the average person. His book, Smarter Retirement Planning is a prime example of his giving nature. He uses this platform to teach others how to look at money, wealth, and retirement differently. This book empowers people to take control in order to gain financial freedom.

— Andy W - Speaker, Author

This endorsement is provided by a non-client of the financial advisor, and no compensation was provided directly or indirectly. This endorsement is not a guarantee of future performance or investment success, and the endorsement may not be representative of the experience of other customers. Please visit BrokerCheck (https://brokercheck.finra.org) to see more on the background of this professional.

TABLE OF CONTENTS

Important Disclosures

The information provided in this material is for educational purposes only and is not intended as investment, tax, or legal advice. Examples and illustrations are hypothetical and for informational purposes only; they do not represent actual results and are not guarantees of future performance.

Investing involves risk, including the possible loss of principal. Past performance is not indicative of future results. There is no assurance that any investment strategy will be successful.

Market conditions, interest rates, and other factors can change over time and may affect outcomes.

Tax and legal considerations vary by individual circumstances. You should consult with a qualified tax advisor, attorney, or financial professional before making decisions related to your personal situation.

References to third-party companies, products, or services (e.g. SSA.gov, Kiplinger, Investopedia) are provided for informational purposes only and do not constitute endorsement or recommendation. We are not affiliated with these organizations.

This material does not constitute an offer to buy or sell any security or investment product. All investments should be made based on your objectives, risk tolerance, and financial situation.

Converting from a traditional IRA to a Roth IRA is a taxable event.

The cost and availability of life insurance depend on factors such as age, health, and the type and amount of insurance purchased. Before implementing a strategy involving life insurance, it would be prudent to make sure that you are insurable by having the policy approved. As with most financial decisions, there are expenses associated with the purchase of life insurance. Policies commonly have mortality and expense charges. In addition, if a policy is surrendered prematurely, there may be surrender charges and income tax implications.

The opinions contained in this material are those of the author. This information is from sources believed to be reliable, but Cetera Wealth Services, LLC cannot guarantee or represent that it is accurate or complete.

INTRODUCTION
THE VALUE OF THINKING LIKE A FINANCIAL ADVISOR

Many people go through life making financial decisions without a clear plan. They save when they can, invest in what sounds good, and hope for the best in retirement. Often, the easiest option in the 401(k) is chosen, frequently the one with the highest recent return, and then left untouched for years. That approach can create uncertainty, especially when the paycheck stops. An alternative approach is to use a structured way of thinking about money, one that focuses on planning ahead, understanding tradeoffs, and adjusting as life changes. This kind of framework helps reduce guesswork and emotional decision-making. It does not rely on perfect timing or special investments. It relies on process.

You do not have to become a financial advisor to benefit from this approach. Learning to think this way can help bring more structure and clarity to financial decisions and may reduce the likelihood of common mistakes over time. This mindset is not just about knowledge; it emphasizes structure, habits, and perspective. Most advisors do not rely on special or exclusive investments. Much of the value comes from using a framework that helps people stay focused, clear-headed, and adaptable as circumstances change.

COMMON RETIREMENT MISSTEPS

Most retirement mistakes are not caused by laziness or a lack of intelligence. They happen because people are forced to make complex decisions without enough structure, support, or long-term perspective.

13

Here are some common missteps often seen in practice and why they may matter.

- Not having a plan
  If you do not know where you are going, any road will take you there. A plan can give your money direction and purpose. Without one, you may end up making decisions that feel right in the moment but lead to trouble later.
- Ignoring risk
  Markets go up and down. Inflation reduces your purchasing power. Taxes can take more than expected. A good plan does not eliminate risk, but it can prepare you for it and help you manage it over time.
- Overlooking taxes
  Another common mistake is overlooking the role of taxes. The order and timing of withdrawals, how different accounts are taxed, and the use of tools like Roth conversions can make the materially affect how long your money lasts. A good plan considers not just how much you have, but how much you get to keep after taxes.
- Underestimating costs
  Healthcare, taxes, and life's unexpected events can derail even the best savings strategy. Many people focus on building their nest egg, but forget to account for what it will actually cost to live the life they want.
- Failing to plan for the unexpected
  Planning also falls short when people ignore the need to protect against life's big risks. Unexpected healthcare costs, the need for long-term care, or the loss of a spouse's income can all derail an otherwise solid retirement plan. Insurance and risk management are not exciting, but they are often the difference between a secure retirement and a fragile one.

- Letting emotions drive decisions
  Fear and greed often lead to poor timing of decisions.
  Investors panic when markets drop or chase returns after a
  hot streak. Many advisors try to avoid these traps by
  sticking to a defined process. You can do the same, but it
  takes discipline and structure.

These mistakes are not uncommon, but they are avoidable. The sooner you recognize them, the easier it becomes to course correct. Thinking like a financial advisor means having a system that helps you avoid the most damaging choices, especially the ones that feel right in the moment but cause harm down the road.

WHERE EVEN SMART INVESTORS STRUGGLE

Managing your own finances can be rewarding. For many people, it can offer a sense of control, lower costs, and personal satisfaction. And in truth, it is possible to manage your own retirement plan successfully if you are aware of what needs to be done and are willing to commit the time and effort it takes to do it well.

But that is where things can get complicated.

Retirement planning is not just about picking good investments or maxing out your 401(k). It is about knowing how all the pieces fit together over time. It can be easy to overlook key areas that have long-term consequences. Think of it like doing your own plumbing. You might be able to follow instructions and get the basics in place, but if something goes wrong, the cleanup can be messy, expensive, and far more complicated than it looked at first.

One common sign that someone may be in over their head is when they stop asking questions. People managing their own retirement planning may not always realize what they do not know, or they assume that success in one part of their financial life automatically translates to retirement expertise. If someone cannot explain why they made an investment, how it fits into a larger plan, or what would cause them to sell it. That can signal a gap in the overall process. Other signs include uncertainty around required minimum distributions, confusion about how to generate income from different types of accounts, or a lack of strategy when coordinating withdrawals across tax-deferred, taxable, and Roth accounts.

A common pattern is confidence that is not backed by a clear process. People may believe they are diversified, but they may not be sure what that really means. They say they have never had an investment go against them, which often means they are overlooking or forgetting something. They trust they are making logical decisions, but when markets fall, they may react emotionally. That is more about human nature than a personal flaw. It is also why structured planning relies heavily on habits and process.

This book is not here to talk you out of doing it yourself. But rather to show you how much goes into a well-built retirement strategy. If you are up for the challenge, you deserve to do it with clarity. And if you realize it is more than you want to take on alone, you will be better prepared to find the right kind of help.

WHAT SHAPES A WELL-BUILT RETIREMENT STRATEGY

Many people think financial advisors are just investment pickers. And while portfolio management can be part of what advisors do, it is only one piece of a much larger picture. Much of the value happens outside the portfolio, in the planning, decision-making, and conversations that help turn savings into a working retirement strategy.

A big part of our role is helping people figure out how to live off their money in retirement. This involves more than just choosing investments. It may include coordinating multiple moving parts to help make sure your plan holds up over time. Some of the key areas typically involved include:

- Deciding where to take income from and in what order

- Coordinating withdrawals across IRAs, Roth IRAs, brokerage (taxable), and savings

- Using tax planning to help reduce lifetime tax bills

- Modeling different retirement income scenarios

- Managing risk through stress testing and long-term forecasting

- Clarifying what "enough" looks like, so you can make decisions with confidence

When markets are rising and everything feels stable, it is often easier for most people to stay the course. When markets fall or unexpected events shake things up, emotions tend to surface and decisions can feel more urgent. That is often when behavior matters most. In practice, this is why structured conversations, plan reviews, and decision frameworks are commonly used to help slow things down and reduce the risk of making costly decisions driven by fear. Managing those moments independently can be challenging, especially when emotions are pushing for action.

Planning is not just about the numbers. It is about having the structure and perspective to navigate uncertainty. This emphasis on preparation and process is common in professional planning and is a theme woven throughout this book.

WHO THIS BOOK IS FOR

This book is written for people who want to make smarter financial decisions as they prepare for and live through retirement. Maybe you are a hands-on investor who wants to stay in control but work more strategically. Maybe you are someone who has done well saving but find yourself unsure how to turn that into a sustainable income. Or maybe you simply want to understand what an experienced advisor would look at so you can ask more informed questions and approach retirement decisions with greater clarity. Wherever you are starting from, this book is designed to help you think more clearly, plan more intentionally, and move forward with purpose.

This book also explores ways to think through how to preserve what you have built and how to pass it on thoughtfully. Estate planning is not just for the wealthy. It is about reducing uncertainty for a spouse, children, or other heirs and helping keep your financial life organized as you move into the next stage.

CHAPTER 1
THE ADVISOR'S MINDSET— PLANNING WITH PURPOSE

Many people go through life making financial decisions without a clear plan. They save when they can, invest in what sounds good, and hope for the best in retirement. They pick the easiest option in the 401(k), or the one with the highest recent return and then rarely look at it again. That's a recipe for stress and uncertainty. Most financial advisors take a more structured approach. They have a system, a methodical way of looking at money, planning for the future, and adjusting as needed. You don't have to become a financial advisor, but if you learn to think like one, you can make smarter decisions, avoid common pitfalls, and build a retirement strategy that works.

UNDERSTANDING THE BIG PICTURE: WHY STRUCTURE MATTERS

One of the most important shifts in managing retirement planning is recognizing that the financial world is not always a level playing field. Information is not distributed evenly, and much of what is readily available is not tailored to individual circumstances. Without context or structure, it can be difficult to separate useful guidance from noise.

Many people end up piecing together decisions from headlines, outdated advice, or what friends and coworkers happen to be doing. Without a clear framework, decisions are more likely to be influenced by emotion, trends, or short-term results. It's also common to remember successes more vividly than setbacks, which can reinforce a false sense of confidence.

A more structured approach focuses on evaluating decisions consistently over time, paying less attention to short-term outcomes and more attention to whether choices align with a thoughtful process. That shift from reaction to structure is what helps bring clarity to long-term planning.

THAT'S THE SHIFT: RELY LESS ON EMOTION AND MORE ON SYSTEMS.

If you're managing your own investments, it helps to build that same kind of repeatable process. One of the ways to start is by writing down your rationale for every investment you make. Before you hit "buy," ask yourself:

- Why this investment?

- What do I expect it to do?

- What would make me sell it?

Documenting your reasoning can give you a way to evaluate your decisions with clarity later, free from the fog of hindsight or emotion. Over time, this can help build discipline and helps you see patterns in your thinking.

A good process will outlast a lucky outcome and may protect you from a costly mistake.

Investing without a process can be like flying blind. You might get lucky for a while, but eventually, the market will humble you. A disciplined, documented approach won't guarantee success, but it gives you a consistent way to learn, adjust, and grow.

Even a well-designed process isn't immune to change. When something in a strategy stops working, whether due to shifts in the market, changes in tax laws, or evolving personal goals, advisors typically revisit the approach rather than sticking with it out of habit. That can involve revising assumptions, improving the framework, or updating the system itself, not just changing investments. The ability to adapt without abandoning a plan is often what separates guesswork from a more disciplined planning approach.

Another key difference often comes down to context. Advisors typically avoid looking at an investment in isolation. Each decision is considered as part of a broader picture, including risk tolerance, time horizon, tax considerations, and future income needs. An investment may look attractive on paper but still be a poor fit for a specific account, portfolio, or financial goal. This kind of situational analysis is common in structured planning approaches, but it can be easy to overlook when decisions are made without a broader framework.

Professionals often rely on a variety of tools to help bring structure and insight to financial planning. These may include retirement income models, Monte Carlo simulations, tax forecasting software, risk assessments, and stress testing. While these tools do not make decisions on their own, they can help evaluate different scenarios more clearly and support decisions based on evidence rather than instinct.

And then there is access. Individual investors can certainly listen to earnings calls and read financial reports. Professional money managers, such as those running mutual funds, pension portfolios, or hedge funds, often have more direct access to company leadership. They may be able to ask questions of senior executives during earnings calls or communicate more directly with investor relations teams. This kind of access does not provide inside information, but it can offer additional context and clarity beyond what is available through public channels alone.

Lastly, many professional advisors are trained to focus on behavioral dynamics, both by observing patterns across many clients and by managing their own decision-making process. Markets are unpredictable, and when emotions run high, it becomes easier for decisions to drift away from long-term plans. In practice, advisors often help reinforce discipline during turbulent periods by revisiting goals, discussing tradeoffs, and slowing the decision-making process. This kind of support can serve as a stabilizing influence when fear or greed begins to take over.

If you are managing your own finances, that kind of behavioral discipline must come from within. It is challenging, but not impossible. Over time, building structure into your process can reduce how much emotion drives decisions in the moment.

You do not need access to everything professionals use, but borrowing elements of structure, process, and discipline can make it easier to stay on track, regardless of how the market behaves.

WHEN GOOD SAVING HABITS AREN'T ENOUGH

It's easy to assume that if you save enough for retirement, the hard part is over. But that's only half the equation. Without good spending habits to match, even a large nest egg can disappear faster than you think.

He was a successful business owner, and she had helped manage their finances well over the years. By the time they retired, they had built up a portfolio well into the six figures. They had done the hard part: they saved diligently and entered retirement in a great position.

But then, the spending started.

At first, it was small indulgences like family vacations, a few celebrations. Then came the real estate: multiple homes in different states, each with maintenance, taxes, and travel costs. They justified keeping the properties because "the kids like to visit once a year." But once-a-year joy became a year-round financial drag.

When we met, they wanted more income from the portfolio, more lifestyle, more comfort, more cash flow. Within about seven years, they had spent down most of what they'd worked decades to build. At one point, they had about $200,000 left and were withdrawing over $40,000 per year. They'd started refinancing properties to pull out cash, essentially trading long-term security for short-term liquidity.

They had great saving habits, but no plan to control spending. Retirement isn't just about building wealth. It's about knowing how to make it last.

WHY "NO PLAN" IS A DANGEROUS PLAN

In my experience, retirement without a plan feels less like a destination and more like a slow drift toward uncertainty. You might have a big balance saved, but without a structure for how to use that money, it can be easy to overspend in the early years and run short when you need it most.

This doesn't happen overnight. It usually starts with something that feels responsible: a celebration, a family trip, maybe buying a second home "for the kids to enjoy." But it snowballs. Each year, the withdrawals get a little bigger, and before long, what looked like a comfortable retirement becomes a math problem with no good answer.

- That's why many advisors tend to approach retirement planning differently. Rather than focusing only on the question, "Do you have enough saved?" they also consider:

- "How much can you safely withdraw each year?"

- "What expenses are wants vs. needs?"

- "What guardrails will keep you on track when emotions take over?"

- "What has changed in your life that we need to account for?"

Thinking like an advisor means treating retirement like a marathon rather than a victory lap. It recognizes that spending decisions matter just as much as saving, and that without ongoing attention, even well-built plans can be tested over time.

If you're managing your own retirement, don't assume that saving was the hard part. The real challenge is making those savings last. That requires a strategy, one that keeps you grounded, helps you say "yes" to the right things, and "not yet" to the things that could throw everything off course.

WHY FOCUS ON HABITS, NOT JUST GOALS?

Most people think of retirement as a number: "If I hit $1 million, I'll be fine." That framing is common, but many advisors approach the question more broadly. It is not just about how much money you have, but how that money will be used over time. A retirement plan typically needs to account for lifestyle, healthcare costs, taxes, and even the legacy you hope to leave behind.

It is also important to understand where savings are held. Assets may be spread across 401(k)s, IRAs, Roth IRAs, savings accounts, CDs, or taxable brokerage accounts. Each plays a different role in the bigger picture of retirement income planning, a topic we will explore in more detail later.

From a planning perspective, many advisors tend to emphasize habits over end goals. Goals describe outcomes, but habits are the actions that move a plan forward. Consistent saving, thoughtful spending, and regular review often matter more over time than hitting a single target once.

For example:

• **Saving for retirement:** Rather than relying on willpower, contributions can be automated so saving happens consistently without constant decision-making.

• **Staying on track:** Regular reviews, whether monthly or quarterly, allow for small adjustments before issues grow into larger problems.

• **Avoiding lifestyle creep:** Spending plans that reflect values, not just income, can help keep progress steady as earnings increase.

These approaches are common in structured planning, but they are not exclusive to professionals. Most people already know what they should be doing. The real challenge is doing it consistently, especially when life gets busy or markets get noisy. That is where habits can make the biggest difference.

Many advisors rely on systems that make good decisions easier to repeat over time. The same kind of structure can be built into your own process as well.

Here are a few habits that can consistently separate those who succeed from those who struggle:

- Pay yourself first. Set up automatic transfers into retirement accounts or savings before you spend anything.

- Schedule regular financial check-ins. Block time on your calendar, just like a dentist appointment, to review your progress.

- Track spending. Not forever, but long enough to notice patterns and make informed choices.

- Revisit your plan. At least once a year, update your strategy based on life changes, market moves, or new goals.

These aren't flashy moves, but they're the foundation. The truth is most of what works in personal finance isn't new. It's been around for decades. Why? Because it works.

If retiring well is your goal, focusing less on a perfect number and more on consistent behaviors can make a meaningful difference over time.

UNDERSTANDING HOW YOU THINK ABOUT INCOME EVEN BEFORE YOU RETIRE

Understanding how you naturally think about income is an important part of retirement planning, even before you stop working. People approach their money in different ways. Some like to organize their savings into mental buckets: what they need soon, what they will need later, and what they plan to use far down the road. Others prefer to think about their portfolio as one large pool, focusing on overall growth and flexibility instead of separating it into categories. Some people stay committed to one style their entire lives, while others shift their preferences as they get closer to retirement. There is no right or wrong approach. What matters is recognizing which style feels most comfortable to you. Later in the book, we will look more closely at these different income preferences, how common they are, and why they play such a meaningful role in long-term retirement decisions.

Most people evaluate financial decisions based on their own experience. If something worked for them, they may assume it was the right path. If something didn't, they may avoid it entirely. That narrow perspective can lead to overconfidence, fear-driven choices, or habits that ignore the bigger picture.

One of the challenges of managing a plan independently is that you only get to see one story: your own. In contrast, professional planning environments involve exposure to many different situations over time. Seeing how a wide range of plans unfold across bull markets, recessions, early retirements, long retirements, market downturns, health events, family changes, windfalls, and slow-but-steady progress can reveal patterns that are hard to recognize from a single experience.

That broader perspective helps highlight what tends to hold up over time, where plans commonly break down, and how decisions made today can ripple years into the future. This kind of wide-lens thinking is often built into structured planning approaches, regardless of who is applying them.

You do not need to see hundreds of plans yourself. That is one of the goals of this book. What matters is learning to step back, zoom out, and evaluate your own decisions within a broader context, rather than relying solely on what has worked for you so far.

Bringing It All Together: Think, Plan, Repeat

If there is one central takeaway from this chapter, it is this: effective planning is less about knowing everything and more about committing to a clear, repeatable process.

Advisors do not have a crystal ball. Markets, tax laws, and life events are inherently unpredictable. Rather than trying to forecast the future, many advisors rely on a framework that emphasizes structure over impulse, habits over hope, and long-term progress over short-term reactions.

If you are managing your own finances, borrowing from that kind of structured approach can be a powerful starting point. Practical ways to apply it include:

- Moving away from gut-driven decisions
- Documenting the reasoning behind choices
- Automating what works consistently
- Reviewing plans periodically and adjusting as circumstances change

Perfection is not required. Consistency tends to matter more over time. That principle shows up often in professional planning, and it is one individuals can apply just as effectively on their own.

In the next chapter, this approach is applied directly to personal finances. We will look at key areas such as income, expenses, debt, savings rate, and emergency reserves, and introduce a framework for evaluating financial health that can help clarify where to begin and which areas may deserve attention.

Thinking more clearly about retirement starts with seeing your full financial picture and being honest about where adjustments may be needed.

CHAPTER 2
DIAGNOSING YOUR FINANCIAL HEALTH WITH INTENTION

When evaluating financial health, advisors typically rely on diagnosis rather than guesswork. The same approach can be useful when reviewing your own finances. Think of it like a medical checkup: understanding where you stand comes before deciding what to do next.

CONDUCTING A FULL FINANCIAL AUDIT

Before making any decisions, you need a clear picture of your financial health. Here's how to conduct a thorough financial audit:

1. **Gather Financial Statements** – Bank, investment, mortgage, loans, etc

2. **List All Sources of Income** – Salaries, pensions, rental income, dividends, side gigs

3. **Track Monthly Expenses** – Break into fixed and variable categories

4. **Calculate Your Savings Rate** – Healthy target: 10-15%

5. **Review Your Debt** – List outstanding debts and prioritize high-interest ones

6. **Check Your Emergency Fund** – Aim for 3–6 months of expenses

To evaluate your financial health thoughtfully, it helps to look at several key areas. Each plays a role in shaping a retirement plan that can adapt as circumstances change. We'll take a closer look at each one so you can work through them step by step and apply a structured approach that advisors commonly use when reviewing financial health.

STEP 1: GATHER YOUR FINANCIAL STATEMENTS

Before you can build a real retirement plan, you need to know what you're working with. This first step is simple but often skipped. Pulling together your financial statements gives you the full picture. It helps you see where you stand today, which is an important starting point.

Think of this as your financial inventory. Without it, you're flying blind. You might think you're in great shape or worse than you really are, but unless you've gathered the data, it's just a guess.

Here's what you'll want to collect:
- Bank account statements (checking, savings, CDs)
- Retirement account statements (401(k), 403(b), IRA, Roth IRA)
- Brokerage accounts and any taxable investment accounts
- Pension statements or benefit estimates
- Social Security statements (you can get this at ssa.gov)
- Mortgage balances and any other loans
- Insurance policies with cash value (life, annuity, etc.)

If you're married, collect this for both of you. You're building a household picture, not just an individual one.

Be on the Lookout for "Forgotten" Assets

It's very common to forget about old accounts. That 401(k) from a job you left ten years ago? It's probably still out there. The life insurance policy your parents helped you open in your twenties? It might have cash value now. Many people also treat Social Security like a surprise bonus rather than part of their plan. I hear things like, "Well, that'll just be extra," but it can be a major piece of retirement income. Ignoring it can create blind spots.

Why This Matters

Not having a complete picture of your finances can lead to real challenges. Forgetting about an account may cause someone to live more conservatively than necessary, while overestimating the value of an asset can lead to overspending. Either situation can introduce unnecessary stress. Advisors often see situations where people plan around the future sale of a business or an expected inheritance, only to discover that the proceeds are smaller than anticipated or not available when needed.

Few situations are more difficult than watching a surviving spouse try to piece together a financial life they were never part of. When one person handles everything, the lack of shared understanding can create confusion and stress at exactly the wrong time. Advisors frequently encounter this dynamic, which is why visibility and shared awareness are emphasized early in the planning process.

Don't Wait for the Perfect Moment

You might feel like things are too messy to tackle. Or maybe you're embarrassed about not having kept better records. Don't let that stop you. You have to start somewhere. There's no better time than right now. This doesn't have to be perfect. Just start pulling things together.

Keep It Simple

Organize your information in a way that works for you. A spreadsheet, a notebook, or even a folder with printed statements. The format doesn't matter. The clarity does. Start by making a list of your accounts and where they are held. Review it annually, or every other year if that feels more realistic. You'll be glad you did.

STEP 2: LIST ALL SOURCES OF INCOME

Once you've gathered your statements and have a handle on your accounts, the next step is to list all your sources of income. This might seem straightforward, but the key is to go a little deeper. You want to know what's coming in, when it starts, and how long it will last.

Start by listing every source of income connected to your household, even if the amount feels small or irregular. This includes money you receive now as well as income you expect to receive in the future, such as:

- Salary or wages
- Business or freelance income
- Rental income
- Pension benefits
- Social Security
- Dividends and interest from investments
- Annuity payments
- Royalties or side income

For each item on your list, note whether it is current (you are receiving it now) or future (you expect to receive it later). Then add the expected start date, and if applicable, an end date. This helps clarify which income sources are dependable today and which ones will play a role later in retirement.

For example:

- Your job income might end when you retire at age 65
- Social Security might begin at 67
- An annuity might pay for 10 years starting at age 70
- A pension may start at 65, but drop by 50% after the pensioner passes away
- Rental income might be current but could stop if you plan to sell the property

Understanding the timing of each source helps you see the full arc of your financial life, not just a snapshot. This exercise is about mapping assets across time.

People generally understand that their paycheck will stop when they retire. The real challenge is understanding how their income will change, not just in amount, but in type, timing, and reliability. This is especially true with things like Social Security, pensions, annuities, and spousal benefits. Many people aren't sure when these benefits begin, how much they'll be, or what happens after one spouse passes away.

This is where a more structured way of thinking becomes especially helpful. When building a plan, advisors generally look beyond simply listing income sources and focus on how those sources function over time. You don't need specialized credentials to apply the same approach. Start by asking practical questions: What income will you have? When will it start? How long will it last? And would it continue for a spouse if something were to happen to you?

Even a basic list that includes this level of detail can put you ahead of the curve. It's not about getting it perfect, it's about being realistic. Understanding the structure and timing of your income can provide useful clarity as you begin shaping a plan that fits your situation.

STEP 3: TRACK MONTHLY EXPENSES

You'd think this one would be obvious. If you're planning for retirement, you need to know what you spend. And yet, it's easy to breeze through this step or give it less attention than it deserves. A lot of people think they already know their expenses. They do the mental math (cable/streaming, cell phone, utilities, mortgage) and then move on. But that approach can miss a lot.

When people estimate their expenses, they often forget irregular costs like annual property taxes, annual or quarterly insurance premiums, or even seasonal spending. They also tend to underestimate the small things that add up: eating out, daily coffee, online subscriptions, or one-off Amazon purchases. It's easy to overlook those when you're not actively tracking.

This isn't about obsessing over every receipt. You don't need to track every dollar unless that's how you're wired. But a rough guess isn't enough either. Retirement planning relies heavily on cash flow. If you don't know how much money is going out the door, how can you know what kind of lifestyle you can support?

A practical approach includes:

- Track your monthly expenses with some level of detail. Use a spreadsheet, budgeting app, or even paper and pen. The method doesn't matter. The method matters less than having a clear view of where your money goes.
- Include non-monthly expenses. List out anything you pay annually, quarterly, or semi-annually, like insurance premiums, property taxes, holiday spending, or memberships. These don't always show up on monthly statements, but they still affect your cash flow.
- Do a full, detailed tracking at least once. Tracking every expense for a full quarter can provide valuable insight. Doing this once while you're working, and again retirement approaches, helps clarify how spending patterns change.

And when you're close to retirement, build a retirement-specific budget. Don't just use your current expenses. Think through what could change:

- Will you still have a mortgage?
- Will your commuting and lunch expenses go down?
- Will healthcare costs go up?
- Will you be traveling more in the early years of retirement?
- Are there new hobbies or home projects you want to take on?

A good retirement budget separates the "must-haves" from the "want-to-haves." You need to know the difference between what you must spend (housing, taxes, insurance, utilities) and what you want to spend (vacations, entertainment, splurges). Both matter, but they need to be understood differently.

This is the kind of structured thinking that underpins a well-built financial plan. Rather than looking at a single number and moving on, the process involves breaking it down, categorizing it, and asking practical questions: What is likely to stay the same? What might change? What is flexible? That approach helps create a plan that reflects real life, not just a spreadsheet.

You don't need to do this every month for the rest of your life. But it does help to go through the exercise with intention. Without that clarity, retirement plans are often built on assumptions, which can create challenges later on.

STEP 4: CALCULATE YOUR SAVINGS RATE

Many people can tell you how much they save each year in dollars. Fewer can say what percentage of their income that savings represents. Looking at savings as a percentage can offer more useful context.

Dollar amounts alone don't tell the full story. A percentage-based savings rate adjusts with income and provides a clearer picture of consistency over time. If income rises, saving as a percentage helps contributions increase automatically. If income falls, it helps clarify how much flexibility exists. In both cases, percentages can make it easier to stay oriented through changes.

When evaluating savings, it helps to look across three key areas:
• Retirement account contributions (401(k), IRA, Roth, etc.)
• Emergency fund savings
• Non-retirement savings (brokerage accounts, CDs, and other after-tax savings)

Start by calculating how much you're saving in total across these buckets. Then divide that by your gross income (not net). This gives you your savings rate.

So what's a good number to aim for? You'll hear a lot of experts suggest saving 10 to 15 percent of your income. Fidelity, for example, recommends working toward a savings rate of 15% of your gross income, including any employer match [1]. That may sound like a lot, especially if you're not close to that today. But here's the good news: you don't have to get there all at once.

If you're just getting started, the first step is simple: contribute enough to your employer plan to get the full match. That's free money, and it's a no-brainer. Once you're doing that, shift your focus to building a solid emergency fund.

After those two basics are in place, here's a strategy I recommend to nearly everyone: increase your savings rate by one percentage point each year. If you're saving 10% of your income this year, bump it to 11% next year, then 12% the year after that until you get to around 15%. This works especially well if you're getting raises each year. You get to keep more, and you save more. It's a win-win.

It's common to worry about starting later than planned or not saving as much as you'd like. In many cases, small, manageable changes can still improve the picture over time. This isn't about assigning blame or creating guilt. It's about recognizing where you are and looking for practical ways to move forward.

Once you retire, your savings rate technically drops to zero. You're no longer contributing to retirement accounts, and that can free up some cash flow. But be careful—it's easy for all of that freed-up money to shift straight into spending. This is where having a clear retirement plan, especially an income plan, becomes essential.

I work with a lot of clients who are excellent savers. Still, the transition from saving to spending isn't always easy. Some retirees remain frugal, holding tightly to long-standing habits. Others see a large account balance and feel a new sense of freedom, sometimes spending more quickly without a clear picture of how long the money needs to last. Neither approach is wrong, but both benefit from thoughtful planning.

This highlights a more structured way of thinking about savings. Rather than focusing only on how much is being saved, it also considers the percentage, the consistency, and whether those habits align with broader goals. Over time, the emphasis shifts toward building sustainable habits, not just reaching a dollar target once and moving on.

You can apply this same thinking to your own situation. Start with your current number. Set a target. Revisit it once a year. And remember that your savings rate isn't just a number — it reflects how you're shaping your future.

STEP 5: REVIEW YOUR DEBT

Debt isn't something to judge. The purpose of reviewing it is to understand how it affects savings, cash flow, and long-term retirement flexibility. Advisors typically approach debt this way, focusing on impact rather than blame.

If you have debt, the goal isn't to feel bad about it. The goal is to understand how it fits into your overall financial picture. It helps to see how different debts influence your ability to save today and generate income in retirement.

Debt becomes a problem when it takes up too much of your monthly cash flow in retirement. If your required payments are high and your savings can't support both the debt and your living expenses, you may not be able to retire comfortably. That's a difficult reality, but it's an important one to face honestly.

At the same time, carrying some debt into retirement can be perfectly fine. It depends on your personal situation. If your savings can support the payments and still allow you to live the way you want, that's your call. There is no one-size-fits-all rule. It all comes back to cash flow.

From a planning perspective, a helpful benchmark is the debt-to-income ratio. A commonly accepted guideline is to keep your total debt payments below 35 percent of your gross income, even in retirement. This is not a hard rule, but it provides a practical way to assess whether debt is taking up too much of your available income [2].

When reviewing debt, advisors typically focus on three key factors:

- The type of debt
- The interest rate
- The required monthly payment

Not all debt is created equal. A low-interest car loan is very different from a high-interest credit card balance. One might make sense to carry, while the other may be draining your resources.

Many retirees still have a mortgage, especially those who locked in low interest rates. From an advisor's perspective, this isn't automatically a red flag. The key is whether the payments fit comfortably within the retirement income plan and allow the person to maintain their desired lifestyle [3].

On the other hand, credit card debt and student loans, including loans cosigned for children, can create an ongoing burden if left unmanaged. These often carry higher interest rates and require closer attention when planning for retirement income [3].

The real issue is not whether you have debt. It is how much income it will take to manage it. If your debt requires a large chunk of your retirement income just to make the payments, that is a sign it may need to be addressed. Otherwise, debt can be just another line item in your retirement budget. Whether you decide to pay it off or keep making payments is up to you. What matters most is that it fits into your overall plan.

To keep it simple, create a spreadsheet or central list that includes:
- The current balance
- The interest rate
- The monthly payment
- The number of months or years left on the loan

Having all of this in one place helps you see the full picture and make more informed decisions moving forward.

STEP 6: CHECK YOUR EMERGENCY FUND

An emergency fund is a cornerstone of financial resilience, both before and after retirement. You need to have cash available to pay for unexpected expenses. It helps keep you from having to sell investments at the wrong time, dip into retirement accounts early, or go into debt when life doesn't go according to plan.

Pre-Retirement: Building the Safety Net

During your working years, the goal is to build a basic cushion to protect against the unexpected. A common recommendation is to have three to six months of essential living expenses saved in a low-risk, easily accessible place such as a savings account or a certificate of deposit. This helps you weather a job loss, medical event, or major repair without disrupting your long-term plans [4].

That said, the challenge I often see is how people define "emergency." Some treat predictable expenses like annual insurance premiums or even buying a new phone, as reasons to dip into their emergency savings. Others simply underestimate what could go wrong. For example, many people don't budget for major home repairs like a new roof or HVAC system, even though those expenses can appear with no warning and carry a five-figure price tag.

Post-Retirement: Adjusting the Strategy

Once you're retired, the role of the emergency fund shifts. There is no paycheck coming in, so cash flow relies heavily on investments, Social Security, and other fixed income. When something breaks or goes wrong, the question becomes: how do you cover it without disrupting your overall retirement income plan?

Many advisors suggest that retirees maintain a larger reserve, typically six to twelve months of expenses. Some even recommend holding up to two years of living expenses in cash or near-cash accounts, especially for those who depend on market-based income sources. This gives you more flexibility and helps you avoid selling investments during a market downturn just to raise cash [5].

The right number is personal. It depends on your lifestyle, your withdrawal strategy, and how much flexibility your other accounts provide.

Common Pitfalls
- Using the fund for non-emergencies
- Not replenishing it after use
- Failing to account for large, irregular costs like home maintenance
- Having too much money tied up in non-liquid accounts

One red flag I look for is when retirees have most or all of their assets in non-liquid investments, such as annuities without flexible access. When an unexpected expense comes up, there may be limited options for handling it smoothly. While annuities and similar tools can serve a purpose, maintaining an accessible emergency fund still plays a critical role.

Best Practices
- Keep your emergency fund in a liquid, low-risk account like a high-yield savings or money market fund
- Include a plan to rebuild it if it gets used
- Review the amount annually or when your situation changes, especially at major life transitions

I tend to view the emergency fund as a tool for flexibility and peace of mind. It does not have to be overly complicated, but it does benefit from being intentional.

Bringing It All Together
Taking a step back to look at the full picture can bring meaningful clarity. By gathering your financial information, reviewing income and expenses, and understanding how debt, savings, and emergency reserves

fit together, you're doing something many people never take the time to do. That clarity can support more intentional decisions and help you plan rather than simply react.

In the next chapter, we'll zoom out even further. You'll use the information you've gathered to organize a clear snapshot of your net worth. This snapshot serves as an important reference point for future retirement decisions, from how much you may need to when stepping away from work becomes realistic. It's not about perfection. It's about seeing where you stand so you can move forward with greater confidence.

References

1. Fidelity Investments. "How much should I save for retirement?" https://www.fidelity.com/viewpoints/retirement/how-much-money-should-I-save

2. National Council on Aging (NCOA). "Understanding Borrowing and Credit When Retirement Planning." https://www.ncoa.org/article/understanding-borrowing-and-credit-when-retirement-planning

3. Mutual of Omaha. "Handling Debt in Retirement." https://www.mutualofomaha.com/advice/financial-planning/build-your-financial-future/handling-debt-in-retirement

4. Ameriprise Financial. "Establishing a Cash Reserve: What It Is and How Much Should You Have" https://www.ameriprise.com/financial-goals-priorities/personal-finance/how-to-establish-a-cash-reserve

5. Real Investment Advice. "The Importance of Emergency Funds in Retirement Planning" https://realinvestmentadvice.com/resources/blog/emergency-funds-in-retirement

CHAPTER 3
BUILDING A ROCK-SOLID
FOUNDATION BEFORE YOU INVEST

Imagine standing before the Leaning Tower of Pisa, its iconic tilt captivating millions of visitors each year. While its slant adds to its charm, it is also a monument to the consequences of a weak foundation. Built in the 12th century on soft, unstable soil, the tower began leaning even before construction was complete. Over the centuries, numerous efforts were made to stabilize it. The largest of those efforts came in the 1990s, when a project costing more than £25 million (over $30 million in U.S. dollars [3]) was launched to prevent collapse. Engineers had to extract soil from beneath the higher side, install steel cables, and carefully adjust the structure's center of gravity. The work took 11 years and still requires ongoing monitoring today [1][2].

Even now, the tower remains upright only because of continuous maintenance and intervention. It is a powerful metaphor for financial planning. A weak foundation may not cause immediate collapse. Like the Tower of Pisa, your financial life may remain standing for decades without appearing to be in danger. However, it is far from stable. One unexpected event, such as job loss, a major medical bill, or a market downturn, can shift the balance and bring everything crashing down.

You can fix a shaky foundation later, just as the engineers did in Pisa. But doing so will cost you more time, money, and effort. Worse yet, while you are busy making those repairs, you may lose valuable opportunities for growth. That is why it is better to build your financial base early, before your investment strategy is fully in motion.

The good news is that building a financial foundation doesn't have to follow a strict sequence. You don't need to wait until all debt is paid off before beginning to invest, or delay insurance decisions until an emergency fund is fully built. Many people work on several areas at the same time. What matters most is avoiding the temptation to skip over foundational pieces in a rush to chase returns.

In this chapter, we'll walk through three foundational elements that are commonly reviewed before shaping an investment strategy:

- **Emergency Funds:** A buffer designed to help absorb unexpected expenses
- **Debt Management:** An approach to managing liabilities that can influence long-term flexibility
- **Insurance Protection:** Tools that can help protect income and assets when life takes an unexpected turn

Together, these elements do more than offer protection. They can contribute to a greater sense of stability and clarity, making it easier to approach long-term investing with intention.

PILLAR 1: EMERGENCY FUNDS — YOUR FIRST LINE OF DEFENSE

Building a financial foundation means being prepared for the unpredictable. One common way to do that is by setting aside a dedicated emergency fund. Not just "extra money in the bank," but a defined, intentional reserve meant to help absorb unexpected expenses when life doesn't go according to plan.

An emergency fund isn't exciting. It's not about high returns or market performance. It's about resilience. Think of it as the financial equivalent of a helmet. You hope you won't need it, but having it in place can make a meaningful difference when something unexpected happens.

Why This Often Comes First

Emergency funds are often addressed early in financial planning because markets and personal emergencies don't operate on the same schedule. If a car breaks down or a job loss occurs during a market downturn, having cash on hand can reduce the need to sell investments at an inopportune time.

An emergency fund can provide flexibility when markets are under stress. It gives investments time to recover and helps reduce the pressure to make decisions driven by fear or urgency. Without that buffer, financial plans may be more vulnerable to short-term disruptions.

As discussed in Chapter 2, many planning frameworks suggest maintaining several months of living expenses in reserve while working, with larger buffers often considered in retirement depending on income sources and lifestyle. The purpose here isn't to prescribe a specific number, but to explain why having that reserve can matter.

Even a well-diversified portfolio may struggle to protect against poor timing when withdrawals are forced. Emergency funds aren't about performance. They're about providing stability when timing matters most.

What Can Happen When This Step Is Overlooked

It's not uncommon for people to treat accounts like a Roth IRA, a home equity line, or a taxable brokerage account as a fallback for emergencies. Others may view loans from a 401(k) as a temporary solution, assuming they're simply borrowing from themselves. In the short term, these approaches can feel convenient.

The challenge is that many of these options come with trade-offs. Access may be limited, withdrawals can trigger taxes or penalties, and timing matters. Selling investments during a market downturn, tapping retirement accounts early, or redirecting contributions to repay a loan can interrupt long-term progress in ways that aren't always obvious at first.

Most people can navigate a single unexpected expense. The risk tends to grow when retirement savings become the primary source of emergency funding. Over time, that pattern can make it harder for long-term plans to stay on track.

Clarifying the Role of an Emergency Fund

An emergency fund serves a specific purpose, and it can be helpful to distinguish it from other types of savings or financial tools.

- It's not meant to cover predictable expenses. Unexpected events are different from irregular but expected costs. Items like holiday spending, routine car maintenance, or annual insurance premiums are usually better handled through separate savings.
- It's different from a Roth IRA. While Roth contributions can be accessed without penalty, using them for emergencies can reduce the long-term benefits those accounts are designed to provide.
- It's not the same as a 401(k) loan. Borrowing from retirement accounts may offer short-term relief, but it can involve trade-offs, such as reduced contributions, missed growth, or repayment challenges if employment changes.
- It's not a substitute for high-interest credit. Relying on credit cards in a crisis can add cost and complexity at an already stressful time.
- It's not an investment account. Emergency funds prioritize availability and stability over growth. The goal is access when needed, not exposure to market fluctuations.

Where to Keep It and Why That Matters

When deciding where to keep emergency savings, accessibility and stability often matter more than return. Common options include:

- **High-yield savings account**

  - Pros: FDIC-insured, easy access, modest interest
  - Cons: Returns may not keep up with inflation
  - Best for: Simple, no-nonsense emergency storage
- **Money market account**

  - Pros: Similar to savings accounts but may offer slightly better rates and limited check-writing
  - Cons: Withdrawal limitations may apply
  - Best for: People who want safety with just a touch more flexibility
- **Short-term CDs or Treasury bills**

- Pros: Safe and can offer slightly better yields if laddered properly
- Cons: Tied up for a set time unless you use a CD or bond ladder
- Best for: Retirees or conservative savers with some flexibility

It's usually best to avoid placing emergency funds in assets like stocks or real estate, where volatility or access restrictions could limit their usefulness in a crisis.

Common Red Flags to Watch For

Certain patterns can signal that an emergency fund may not be serving its intended role. Examples include:

- Regularly dipping into emergency savings for vacations, gifts, or everyday spending

- Using retirement accounts, such as a Roth IRA or 401(k), as a substitute for accessible emergency cash

- Having less than a month of expenses set aside while feeling "invested for the long term"

- Keeping emergency savings in the same account as day-to-day checking, making it easier to access unintentionally

- Relying on credit cards or loans to handle unplanned expenses

These situations aren't about blame. They often indicate that the financial foundation could benefit from some reinforcement before additional layers of complexity are added.

A Simple Self-Check

Ask yourself the following:

1. Do I have at least three months of essential expenses in cash or cash equivalents?

2. Is my emergency fund clearly separated from everyday spending accounts?
3. Have I avoided dipping into it for things that aren't true emergencies?
4. Do I have a plan to replenish it quickly if I ever use it?
5. Could I cover an unexpected $5,000 expense without using debt or withdrawing from retirement?

If any of these answers are "no," it may be time to revisit your emergency planning before taking the next steps.

What About Big Home Repairs?

A common point of confusion is whether large home repairs—like a roof replacement, water heater failure, or HVAC system breakdown—should come from your emergency fund. After all, these costs are big and often urgent.

But here's the key: **home maintenance is not an emergency.** These are predictable, recurring costs of owning a home. Roofs wear out. Furnaces and air conditioners eventually fail. These are expenses you can reasonably anticipate and budget for.

Many financial experts recommend setting aside **1% to 4% of your home's value each year** for maintenance and repairs. On a $300,000 home, that's $3,000 to $12,000 annually [4]. This money should be saved in a separate account—call it your *home maintenance fund*. It gives you a buffer for when the inevitable happens, without draining your emergency cash reserves.

Emergency funds are for the unknown. Think job loss, medical issues, or sudden income disruption. Maintenance funds are for the inevitable. When you keep those categories separate, you protect your financial foundation and avoid shortchanging your safety net.

One Final Thought

Emergency funds aren't built for excitement. They're built for function. Few people feel enthusiastic about letting cash sit in a low-return savings account. But many feel relieved when a hospital bill, roof repair, or job loss comes along and they aren't scrambling to figure out how to pay for it.

An emergency fund can help keep a difficult situation from turning into a financial crisis. You don't build one because you expect to use it. You build it because you might need to, and having that buffer is an important part of a strong financial foundation.

PILLAR 2: DEBT MANAGEMENT—THE SILENT WEALTH KILLER

Many people think about debt in terms of whether they can afford the monthly payment. But in retirement planning, the question becomes how will that debt will impact your future lifestyle and long-term financial security. Debt does not always feel urgent, which is exactly why it can quietly erode your plan if you do not pay attention to it.

Debt is not inherently bad. It can be used wisely and managed well. But when it begins to limit your choices or dominate your cash flow, it can become a threat. Understanding how debt fits into your retirement strategy is one of the more important things you can do before investing or making long-term decisions.

Why Debt Matters More in Retirement

As you approach retirement, the conversation around debt shifts. It is no longer just about whether you can make the payment. It is about whether that payment fits into your future income plan.

During your working years, you have a regular paycheck to manage your obligations. But in retirement, your cash flow may come from a mix of sources such as investments, pensions, Social Security, or annuities. Every dollar used to pay down debt is a dollar that does not support your lifestyle or give you flexibility when life changes.

This is why debt management is one of the three core pillars in building a solid foundation. Ignoring it can put stress on the other parts of your financial plan, especially your ability to cover both fixed and discretionary expenses later in life.

Types of Debt and What to Watch For

Not all debt is equal. Here are a few general principles to help evaluate how debt may fit or not fit into your financial plan.

- **Low-interest mortgage debt** can sometimes be kept in place, particularly if the interest rate is lower than what your conservative investments are currently earning. For example, if your mortgage rate is 3.5 percent and you are earning 5 percent on your savings or short-term investments, it may make sense to continue making regular payments and keep the loan in place. On the other hand, if your investments are earning less than the interest you are paying, or if the debt causes you stress, paying it off may be the better choice. This is not a universal rule. The best choice depends on your personal preferences and investment approach.

- **Auto loans** can be reasonable when they're used intentionally, and the payment fits comfortably within your overall plan. The focus is less on whether the rate is "good" and more on whether the loan supports your cash flow, savings habits, and long-term flexibility.

- **Zero percent financing offers**, including short-term promotions on larger purchases like appliances or furniture, can also be reasonable if they are used intentionally. These arrangements can make sense when the purchase is necessary, the payments are manageable, and the balance is paid in full before interest applies. The risk comes when promotional terms are overlooked or when multiple offers begin to overlap.

- **Home equity loans** can create flexibility when used carefully, but they reduce future options and should be evaluated as part of your broader income plan. This is especially important if you are relying on the equity in your home as part of your retirement funding.

- **High-interest debt**, such as credit cards, often poses the greatest threat to your long-term financial health. It can grow quickly and reduce your ability to invest or build reserves. When possible, this type of debt should be addressed early.

Rather than labeling debt as good or bad, a more practical approach is to ask this question: Can you reasonably expect to earn more on your savings or investments (after taxes) than the interest you are paying on your debt? If not, paying down the debt may provide a more predictable return than any investment would. But again, the right answer depends on your situation, risk tolerance, and retirement goals.

Debt-to-Income Guidelines

In Chapter 2, we introduced a helpful benchmark: keeping total debt payments below 35 percent of gross income, especially as retirement approaches. This is not a strict rule, but it is a useful threshold. If your monthly obligations are consuming more than a third of your income, your financial flexibility may be at risk.

As you get closer to retirement, it is often wise to aim for a lower ratio. A more manageable level of fixed expenses helps ensure that your retirement income can stretch further and respond better to unexpected changes.

It is not always necessary to be completely debt-free in retirement. Some people maintain a mortgage or other manageable debts and still retire comfortably. What matters is whether those debts fit into your retirement income plan and allow you to live the lifestyle you want without unnecessary stress.

Mortgage Decisions: Pay Off or Keep Paying?

Many people nearing retirement ask whether they should pay off their mortgage. Several factors are important to consider.

For some, eliminating the mortgage brings peace of mind and reduces required monthly outflows. For others, particularly those with low fixed rates and a well-structured investment approach, keeping the mortgage allows assets to remain invested and potentially grow.

One question to ask is whether your current investments are earning more than the interest you are paying on the mortgage, once taxes and fees are considered. If they are, and you are comfortable with some market risk, keeping the mortgage may be appropriate. If not, or if you value certainty over potential growth, paying off the debt could make more sense.

There is no one-size-fits-all solution. These decisions work best when viewed as part of a complete income strategy that accounts for tax implications, liquidity, and long-term goals.

Balancing Debt Repayment and Retirement Savings

If you have debt and are also trying to save for retirement, the order of operations matters.

The first priority should be to contribute enough to your workplace retirement plan to receive the full employer match. This is often referred to as "free money" because it is part of your compensation. Missing it can create a gap that is hard to make up later.

After that, it may be best to focus on reducing high-interest debt. This improves your monthly cash flow and reduces future risk. Once the most costly debt is addressed, you can return to increasing your retirement contributions and building investments.

Here is a simple framework:
- Build an emergency fund
- Contribute to your retirement plan enough to get the full match
- Pay down high-interest debt
- Continue investing once the debt burden is manageable

This balanced approach helps you avoid extremes. You are not ignoring long-term growth, but you are also not dragging a financial anchor behind you.

A Self-Assessment for Debt Readiness

Ask yourself the following questions:

- Do I know the total amount of debt I have, including interest rates and repayment timelines?
- Is this debt manageable based on my projected retirement income?
- Will these payments affect my ability to cover essential expenses?
- Is my investment strategy likely to outperform the interest I am paying?
- Have I planned for this debt to continue—or end—before I retire?

This exercise is not about eliminating all debt. It is about understanding its role in your plan and making decisions that support your long-term goals.

Debt may not be the most urgent part of your financial life today, but it is often one of the most impactful. Taking the time to understand where you stand can meaningfully influence how confident and prepared you feel as you move toward retirement.

PILLAR 3: INSURANCE PROTECTION — GUARDING AGAINST LIFE'S BIG RISKS

Many people view insurance as a necessary evil. It often feels like an expense rather than a benefit. And if everything goes well, it can feel like money wasted. Still, insurance is one of the primary tools used to help reduce the financial impact of major, unexpected events. When structured thoughtfully, it serves as more than a safety net. It plays an important role in supporting long-term financial stability.

Insurance isn't designed to build wealth. Its purpose is to help protect what you've already built. It tends to be most effective when coverage aligns with the specific risks you face at different stages of life.

Life Insurance: Needs Change Over Time

One of the most common planning gaps I see is people carrying too little life insurance during the years when they need it most. If you have children, a spouse, and a mortgage, your financial obligations tend to be significant. The loss of your income would have a real, lasting impact on the household you leave behind. Yet many people determine how much coverage to buy based on what they can afford in monthly premiums, rather than what their family would actually need.

The right amount of life insurance varies depending on your income, your spouse's earning capacity, the age of your children, and other factors. For families in their 30s or 40s, this amount can reach seven figures, particularly when children are young and support needs extend for many years. That is the kind of math that should drive the insurance decision, not just what a policy costs per month.

Life insurance conversations shouldn't stop with income alone. In many families, one spouse earns less or doesn't earn income at all yet plays a central role in daily life. They're the one handling school drop-offs, managing schedules, keeping the household moving, and often holding everything together. If that person were suddenly gone, the loss wouldn't just be emotional. It would change routines, responsibilities, and the way the surviving spouse has to navigate everyday life. That's why life insurance for a non-working or lower-earning spouse isn't about putting a dollar value on those roles. It's about giving the family time, options, and space to adjust without feeling forced into immediate decisions during an already overwhelming moment.

As people get older, those needs decline. You may no longer need to support children, and your mortgage may be nearly paid off. At that point, the question becomes whether your spouse or dependents would experience a meaningful drop in lifestyle if you passed away. That may call for a smaller policy or possibly no policy at all.

One type of policy that can still have value later in life is a small whole life policy designed to help cover funeral and end-of-life expenses. A traditional funeral today may cost around $12,000. Two or three decades from now, that number could reach $30,000 or more. Having coverage in place for those costs can help spare family members from added financial stress during an already difficult time.

Not all permanent policies are structured the same way. Many whole life policies require premiums to be paid for life, which can become burdensome later on. In my experience, limited-pay designs such as 7-pay or 10-pay policies are often chosen by people who want to handle these costs intentionally while they're still working, rather than leaving the decision for later. By funding the policy over a defined period, the coverage can remain in force without ongoing premiums in retirement.

That said, these policies benefit from careful design and periodic review. Poor structuring or lack of monitoring can create issues years down the road, sometimes at the very point when people assume coverage will be there. This is why reviewing life insurance over time and ensuring it continues to align with your goals remains an important part of long-term planning.

Disability Insurance: Often Overlooked, Often Needed

If you are working, your most valuable asset may be your income. Disability insurance is designed to protect that income if illness or injury prevents you from earning. Despite its importance, a lot of people are underinsured in this area.

Many rely solely on group disability coverage through their employer. While this is a good start, group coverage is often limited. It may only cover a portion of income and may not include bonuses, commissions, or income from multiple sources. In some cases, additional coverage beyond the base policy may be needed to better align protection with actual income.

Disability risk is higher than many people assume. According to the Social Security Administration, more than one in four of today's 20-year-olds will become disabled before reaching retirement age [5]. A long-term disability can be financially devastating, especially if it occurs during your peak earning years.

This is an area where professional guidance is especially important. Disability insurance is complex, definitions of disability vary by policy, and small details can determine whether a claim is paid. I believe that anyone evaluating disability insurance should work with someone who understands this space well. Your income is too important to leave potential gaps unexamined.

Long-Term Care Insurance: A Silent Threat to Retirement Savings

Few risks drain retirement savings as quickly as the cost of long-term care. If you need help with daily activities and require full-time nursing or in-home care, the bills add up fast. In 2024, the national median cost of a private room in a skilled nursing facility rose to $127,750 per year [6]. Many people remain in care for several years. Without insurance, those expenses come directly from your savings.

Roughly 70 percent of adults age 65 and older will need some type of long-term care during their lifetime [7]. That is not a rare risk. It is something most retirees will face in some form.

Long-term care insurance is often overlooked in retirement planning. While traditional policies still exist, many people today also explore life insurance with long-term care riders. These hybrid policies can provide access to care benefits while also offering a death benefit if care is never needed.

Long-term care insurance is notoriously complex. Premiums, benefit periods, elimination periods, inflation riders, and daily benefit amounts all need to be evaluated carefully. In my view, this is an area where most people benefit from guidance rather than trying to navigate the options on their own. If you are considering a policy or wondering whether one makes sense, it's important to work with someone who understands long-term care coverage, the marketplace, and how these decisions fit into your overall financial picture.

Long-term care decisions can have meaningful financial and lifestyle implications. Approaching them thoughtfully can help support greater independence and reduce the risk of unexpected strain later in retirement.

Medicare and Health Insurance: Know Your Options

As retirement approaches, health insurance planning becomes critical. Medicare is not one-size-fits-all. There are different parts, different supplement options, and different costs depending on what you choose. Picking the wrong plan can lead to coverage gaps or unnecessary out-of-pocket expenses.

This is another area where guidance matters. There are professionals who specialize in helping retirees compare Medicare Advantage plans, Medigap options, and Part D drug coverage. The system is complicated, and mistakes are costly. It is worth taking the time to understand your options before your 65th birthday.

Property and Liability Insurance: Often Overlooked

Your home, vehicles, and liability coverage are all part of your broader financial safety net. Yet these policies are often set once and then left untouched for years, even as life circumstances and costs change.

One issue that comes up frequently is homeowners being underinsured relative to current replacement costs. Building materials and labor expenses have risen over time, which means older policy limits may no longer reflect what it would actually cost to rebuild. If coverage is based on outdated estimates, gaps can appear when they are least expected. For example, if rebuilding a home would cost $400,000 but the policy only provides $250,000 in coverage, the remaining difference would fall on the homeowner.

Umbrella insurance, which provides extended liability protection above your home and auto policies, is another area often missed. For a relatively small premium, it can protect you from major legal or financial claims that fall outside of standard coverage limits.

The lesson here is not that you need to constantly shop insurance. It is that coverage should generally keep pace with your financial life. As your home value, net worth, and income change, your protection should change with it.

A Final Word on Insurance

Insurance is not exciting. It is not about building wealth. It is about helping protect the wealth and plans you are already building. When you need insurance, it matters that coverage is in place and functions as intended. That tends to happen when policies are understood, reviewed periodically, and thoughtfully integrated into your overall plan.

You don't need to become an expert in every type of insurance. But having a clear understanding of what you're protected against—and where gaps may exist—can make a meaningful difference. That level of awareness can put you ahead of the curve and better prepared as your financial life evolves.

My Experience with Homeowners Insurance

A few years ago, I bought a new home. As part of setting up my coverage, I asked the insurance agent to get a rebuild estimate from the underwriter. They came back with a number around $120 per square foot.

Even at the time, I knew that estimate was likely outdated. I had been watching construction costs rise and believed the true cost was closer to $225 to $250 per square foot. Had I accepted the original figure and something happened, I could have been left underinsured by hundreds of thousands of dollars.

I pushed back, had the policy updated, and raised the insured value to better reflect the cost of rebuilding. That matters because many homeowners don't realize that when coverage falls short, some policies may reduce the payout even in the event of a total loss. It's not just about having coverage. It's about having enough of it.

This is a good example of why periodically reviewing homeowners insurance can be important. Rather than assuming the number on your policy is accurate, it's worth asking how it was calculated, checking local building costs, and getting clarification when something doesn't seem right. In some cases, a brief conversation can help avoid a costly gap later on.

WHEN ARE YOU READY TO INVEST?

After all the diagnostic work, planning conversations, and foundational pieces covered in this chapter, it's natural to want to start investing. That's often where people want to begin. But in practice, effective investing usually doesn't start with picking stocks or choosing mutual funds. It starts with being ready.

So what does "ready to invest" really look like? It's not about timing the market or guessing the next big thing. Readiness is about preparation. It's about knowing where you stand and having basic systems in place so you're not building on sand. It means your accounts are set up, you've taken time to understand your financial picture, and you have a sense of where you want to go. Most importantly, it means you're not jumping into the markets simply because someone told you that's what responsible people do. You've paused, looked around, and made a plan.

Before you dive too far into investing, there are a few basics worth checking off first:

- **You have an emergency fund** that can cover at least three to six months of living expenses
- **You've addressed your high-interest debt**—either by eliminating it or having a realistic plan to pay it off
- **You've reviewed your risk protection**, including life, disability, and long-term care insurance, so that your plan can survive the unexpected

You can do more than one thing at a time. For example, I always encourage people to contribute enough to their 401(k) to get the full employer match. That's free money, and it's a rare opportunity you can't recapture later. Once that's in place, you can continue improving your financial foundation alongside building your investments.

A mistake I see fairly often is people putting every dollar they can into the market without a clear sense of why. They've heard the message repeatedly: "You need to invest. You need to save. The earlier, the better." And while that message isn't wrong, it's incomplete. Investing without a plan is like buying lumber and nails before you've drawn up the blueprint for your house.

Before you invest, it helps to know what you're building and what that money is meant to support.

After working through the material in this chapter, you should have a clearer sense of where you stand and what needs to be in place before investing becomes the focus. Taking the time to understand your cash flow, your debts, and your risks creates a stronger foundation for the decisions that come next. That groundwork matters more than most people realize.

In the next chapter, we'll begin shaping your retirement savings strategy. Not just saving more but saving with purpose. Not just growing wealth but building a plan designed to support you both on the way to retirement and throughout it.

With the foundation in place, the focus can now shift to how you invest and how those choices fit into the bigger picture.

References

1. BBC. *Leaning Tower of Pisa mystery finally solved by scientists*. BBC Newsround, December 2022. https://www.bbc.co.uk/newsround/64104179

2. Greenberger, A. *The Leaning Tower of Pisa has stopped moving for the first time in 20 years*. Artnet News, June 2023. https://news.artnet.com/art-world/leaning-tower-of-pisa-reduced-tilt-2235641

3. MeasuringWorth. *Exchange rate data for 1990s British Pound to U.S. Dollar*. MeasuringWorth.com. https://www.measuringworth.com/datasets/exchangepound/

4. MoneyFit. *How to Build a Home Repair Savings Fund*. MoneyFit.org. https://www.moneyfit.org/essential-home-repair-savings-guide

5. *Social Security Administration. Disability Benefits (Publication No. 05-10029). U.S. Social Security Administration, January 2024, p. 1. https://www.ssa.gov/pubs/EN-05-10029.pdf*

6. CareScout. *Cost of Care 2024 Report*. https://www.carescout.com/cost-of-care

7. Administration for Community Living (ACL). *How Much Care Will You Need?* https://acl.gov/ltc/basic-needs/how-much-care-will-you-need

CHAPTER 4
CRAFTING A BULLETPROOF
RETIREMENT SAVINGS STRATEGY

Once you have a solid financial foundation, the next step is creating a retirement savings strategy that can stand the test of time. Many people contribute to a 401(k) or IRA without fully understanding how these accounts work or whether they're maximizing their potential.

What accounts should I be using? How much should I be saving? How do I choose between Traditional and Roth? What about brokerage accounts or annuities? These are the kinds of questions that can help bring clarity and direction to long-term financial decisions.

This chapter breaks down how to build a savings strategy that goes beyond "just save more." That means knowing where to put your money, when to use tax-deferred versus Roth accounts, how to avoid future tax traps, and how to create flexibility in your retirement income plan.

Thinking like an advisor means stepping back and building a plan with structure. It means being intentional about which accounts you fund, how those choices affect taxes, and how much flexibility you'll have later. It also means avoiding common pitfalls, like missing a 401(k) match, relying on only one type of account, or overlooking the tax impact of withdrawals.

Let's walk through it step by step. The goal is not to turn you into a financial professional. It's to help you think like one when it comes to saving for retirement.

THE RETIREMENT SAVINGS TOOLKIT: 401(K), IRA, ROTH IRA, AND MORE

When people step back to think seriously about retirement savings, the conversation usually doesn't start with product recommendations or stock picks. It often starts with a simple review:

- Do you have a 401(k) at work?
- What other savings vehicles have you already opened?
- Are you contributing consistently, and how are those contributions structured?

Many people already have something started. But even those who have saved diligently often haven't optimized where or how they're saving. It's not just about how much is in an account. It's also about how those dollars are taxed now, how they may be taxed later, and what flexibility that creates for income in retirement.

TRADITIONAL VS. ROTH: TAX NOW OR TAX LATER?

The first major distinction in retirement accounts is straightforward:

- **Traditional 401(k) or IRA**: You contribute pre-tax dollars, reducing your taxable income today. But you'll pay taxes on every dollar you withdraw in retirement.
- **Roth 401(k) or Roth IRA**: You pay taxes on your income now, but the money grows tax-free and withdrawals in retirement are also tax-free.

There's no one-size-fits-all answer. That's why building a mix of traditional and Roth accounts can add flexibility over time. Especially for higher-income earners, building up traditional and Roth accounts in parallel can give you more control over your tax situation later.

The basic tradeoff is this: traditional accounts save you taxes now; Roth accounts save you taxes later. If you have a mix of both, you gain the ability to choose which account to draw from in retirement based on your needs, tax brackets, and changes in the law.

WHY TAX DIVERSIFICATION MATTERS

Tax laws change. Retirement income needs vary. Having a variety of account types can give you options when it's time to turn your savings into income. Areas that often come into play include:

- **Medicare IRMAA brackets**: Higher income in retirement can result in higher Medicare premiums
- **Social Security taxation**: The more taxable income you have, the more of your Social Security benefit becomes taxable
- **Required Minimum Distributions (RMDs)**: Starting at age 73 (per SECURE Act 2.0), traditional accounts force withdrawals whether you need the money or not

Building a diversified mix of traditional, Roth, and taxable savings can help control how much taxable income you report in retirement, and when you report it.

COMMON RETIREMENT SAVINGS PITFALLS

One issue that comes up frequently is using retirement accounts as an emergency fund. This isn't limited to new or lower-income savers. It happens across income levels. A sudden expense arises, and without adequate cash reserves, people tap into a 401(k) or IRA. The consequences can be steep: taxes, penalties, and missed growth. These accounts are designed for long-term goals, not short-term problems.

Another common pattern is failing to increase savings over time. Many people set a contribution amount early in their careers and rarely revisit it. Small, steady increases can make a meaningful difference over time. Even a one-percent annual increase can compound without requiring major lifestyle changes.

A final area that often gets overlooked is the long-term impact of large traditional account balances. As people reach their 70s and 80s, required minimum distributions can grow substantially, sometimes forcing withdrawals beyond what's actually needed. That additional income can push tax brackets higher, increase Medicare premiums, and reduce overall tax efficiency. Addressing this earlier, through account diversification or gradual Roth conversions during lower-income years, can help reduce that pressure later on.

Smart Strategies That Support Long-term Flexibility

A thoughtful savings strategy doesn't wait until retirement to address tax and income planning. Instead, it considers these issues gradually over time. Common approaches include:
- Contributing to both traditional and Roth accounts when possible
- Using backdoor Roth IRAs when income exceeds direct contribution limits
- Considering partial Roth conversions before required minimum distributions begin
- Avoiding over-reliance on any single account type

This isn't just about growing savings. It's about shaping retirement income in a way that aligns with your lifestyle and helps reduce avoidable tax drag. A flexible approach creates more control over how and when income is generated, which can support a plan designed to carry you not just to retirement, but through it.

Maximizing Tax Efficiency: Save Smart, Not Just More

Once you're consistently saving for retirement, the next step is to make sure you're saving smart. Tax efficiency isn't just for high-net-worth investors. It's one of the more commonly overlooked advantages for people who understand how to use the system.

Advisors generally consider more than just how much is being saved. They also think about where savings are held and what is invested in across different types of accounts. That's where tax efficiency comes into play.

FUNDING ORDER: A COMMON PLANNING FRAMEWORK

When deciding where to direct retirement savings, it can help to think in terms of priority rather than perfection. While no single order fits everyone, many planning frameworks follow a similar sequence:

1. **401(k) up to the employer match** – Employer matching contributions are one of the few guaranteed returns available, which is why they're often prioritized early.

2. **Roth IRA or Traditional IRA (depending on income and eligibility)** – These accounts can offer meaningful tax advantages and additional flexibility outside of an employer plan.

3. **Additional 401(k) contributions** – Once the match and IRA options are addressed, increasing 401(k) contributions can help accelerate long-term savings.

4. **Taxable brokerage accounts** – After tax-advantaged accounts are well funded, taxable accounts can provide flexibility for goals that fall outside traditional retirement timelines.

5. **Health Savings Account (HSA)** – If available, HSAs offer a unique combination of tax-deductible contributions, tax-free growth, and tax-free withdrawals for qualified medical expenses, making them a valuable planning tool for healthcare costs later in life.

If your employer offers both Traditional and Roth 401(k) options, splitting contributions between the two can help create tax diversification. For example, allocating contributions across both types may provide some tax savings today while also building tax-free income for the future. Many people are surprised to learn their plan even includes a Roth option, so it's worth reviewing the details of what's available.

This type of approach isn't about finding a perfect order. It's about building balance. Pre-tax contributions can help today, while Roth and after-tax savings create flexibility later. Over time, that balance can make your overall strategy more resilient.

ASSET LOCATION: THE OVERLOOKED TAX STRATEGY

Not all accounts are created equal when it comes to taxation. Some investments generate regular income, such as bonds or dividend-paying stocks. Others grow over time and primarily produce capital gains, such as exchange-traded funds (ETFs) or mutual funds. Where you place each type of investment can make a meaningful difference.

One common way to think about asset location looks like this:

• **Tax-deferred accounts (Traditional IRA or 401(k))** are often well suited for income-producing investments such as bonds, real estate investment trusts (REITs), and actively managed mutual funds. Because taxes are deferred until withdrawal, these accounts can help shield you from annual tax exposure.

• **Tax-free accounts (Roth IRA or Roth 401(k))** are often used for higher-growth assets such as individual stocks or equity-focused funds. Since qualified withdrawals are tax-free, long-term growth in these accounts can be especially valuable.

• **Taxable brokerage accounts** are commonly used for tax-efficient investments like index funds, ETFs, or individual stocks intended for long-term holding. These investments may generate minimal annual tax impact and can benefit from favorable capital gains treatment.

This is what is meant by asset location. It's different from asset allocation. It's not about what percentage you invest in stocks or bonds, but where you hold those investments based on their tax impact.

What Is Tax Drag?

Tax drag is the erosion of investment returns caused by taxes on dividends, interest, and capital gains. Even small annual taxes can quietly eat away at your long-term growth.

For example, holding a high-turnover mutual fund in a taxable account means you may owe taxes on gains each year, even if you haven't sold anything. That reduces your compounding potential over time.

Tax drag can often be managed by:

- Favoring individual stocks, index funds and ETFs in taxable accounts
- Using tax-deferred or tax-free accounts for less efficient assets
- Being aware of large unrealized capital gains before making changes

Even reinvesting dividends in a taxable account can create tax liabilities year after year. These costs are often invisible until you add them up over decades.

Mistakes to Watch For

Here are some common issues to watch for:

- **Overconcentration in illiquid assets**. Some investors have most of their assets tied up in fixed or variable annuities or other illiquid investments. Accessing funds can be difficult or expensive. Having too much in these illiquid investments can limit flexibility when needs arise.
- **Unrealized capital gains with no exit plan**. It's possible to build up significant gains in individual stocks or funds without thinking through how or when that money may be needed. When the time comes to sell, the result can be a steep tax bill and limited options.
- **No plan for withdrawals**. Without a mix of account types, it becomes harder to manage taxable income. Large balances in tax-deferred accounts can lead to higher required minimum distributions later in life, forcing withdrawals that may increase tax exposure and Medicare costs.
- **Ignoring Roth 401(k) availability**. Many employees default to traditional 401(k) contributions without realizing a Roth option may be available. A blended approach can create more control over taxes in retirement.

ADVANCED, YET PRACTICAL STRATEGIES

Even without being a tax expert, there are practical strategies you can apply:

- **Tax-loss harvesting**. Selling investments that have dropped in value can offset gains elsewhere. Up to $3,000 of losses can also offset ordinary income, and unused losses can be carried forward.
- **Capital gains planning**. You can reduce taxes by spreading gains over several years, selling during low-income years, or pairing gains with harvested losses.
- **Watch the wash sale rule**. If you sell a security at a loss and repurchase the same or a similar investment within 30 days, the IRS disallows the loss.

INHERITED IRAS AND THE 10-YEAR RULE

A new wrinkle in retirement tax planning came with the passage of the SECURE Act and its follow-up, SECURE Act 2.0. For non-spouse beneficiaries who inherit IRAs, the old "stretch IRA" strategy, which allowed required minimum distributions (RMDs) to be spread over a lifetime, is largely gone. Now, for most people, the rule is straightforward: the account must be emptied within ten years.

However, it's not as simple as waiting until year ten. Under current IRS guidance, many non-spouse beneficiaries are required to take annual RMDs during the ten-year period, even though the entire balance must be withdrawn by the end. You can take more than the minimum in any given year, but you generally can't skip distributions entirely and wait until the end.

A more strategic approach often includes the following considerations:

- **Start early**. Waiting too long increases the risk of facing a very large taxable distribution in year 10, especially if the account is sizable or the underlying investments grow significantly.

- **Use the midpoint as a reference.** One commonly used approach is to reassess withdrawals around year five. At that point, dividing the remaining balance by the remaining years can help spread the tax burden more evenly.
- **Coordinate inherited IRA distributions with other savings goals.** If you're not already maximizing contributions to a 401(k) or Roth 401(k), inherited IRA distributions can sometimes be used to cover living expenses while increasing contributions to your own retirement accounts. This can help reduce current taxable income while continuing to build long-term savings.

The right approach depends on several factors: your current income, how much other retirement savings you have, whether you need the inherited IRA money right now, and how large the account is.

These questions often don't come up until someone actually inherits an IRA, but they're worth thinking about in advance, especially if you expect to receive one. Having a plan in place can make a meaningful difference in how much of that inheritance you keep versus how much goes to taxes.

COMMON RETIREMENT SAVINGS MISTAKES

Even diligent savers can fall into traps that undermine their long-term success. Thinking like a financial advisor means spotting the red flags before they turn into real problems. Below are some common retirement savings pitfalls and ways to help reduce their impact .

Mistake #1: Not contributing enough to get the full 401(k) match

This is one of the most common and easily overlooked issues. When someone fails to contribute enough to their 401(k) to earn the full employer match, they are leaving free money on the table.

Let's compare two people: Sarah and Mike. Both work at the same company, earning $60,000 per year. Both age 35. Their employer offers a 100% match on 401(k) contributions up to 5% of their salary.

- Sarah contributes 5% ($3,000 per year), and her employer matches it. Total savings: $6,000 per year for 30 years.
- Mike contributes only 2% ($1,200 per year), so he only gets a $1,200 match. Total savings: $2,400 per year for 30 years

Over 30 years, assuming a 7% annual return:

- Sarah ends up with about $586,000
- Mike ends up with about $234,000

By not contributing enough to get the full match, Mike left approximately $352,000 on the table over his career.

Despite the clear benefits, many workers are not maximizing their 401(k) contributions. In 2023, the average employee contribution rate was 7.8% of salary [1]. Additionally, about 25% of workers miss out on the full employer match, leaving significant retirement funds unclaimed [2].

These figures are hypothetical and for illustrative purposes only. Actual results will vary and are not guaranteed.

Mistake #2: Putting everything into one type of account

Many savers unknowingly create a future problem by putting all of their money into one type of account. This could be:

- All in a Traditional 401(k)
- All in a Roth IRA
- All in a taxable brokerage account
- All in annuities or other illiquid products

This lack of diversity can reduce flexibility once it's time to retire and begin generating income. Retirement income planning is not just about how much you have saved. It is about how you access it. It's about how, when and from where you can access it.

If all your money is in tax-deferred accounts, for example, every dollar you withdraw adds to your taxable income. If it's tied up in annuities or other illiquid investments, access may be limited when you need funds most.

Having a balance between Traditional, Roth, and taxable accounts gives you the ability to manage taxes, help manage Medicare premiums, and smooth your income across different stages of retirement.

Mistake #3: Not thinking about taxes when you withdraw

Retirement planning isn't just about how you save. It's also about how you take money out. A common oversight is overlooking the tax impact of withdrawals. Many investors focus on growing their accounts, only to realize later that taxes can reduce retirement income more than expected.

John and Lisa both retire with $1 million in Traditional 401(k) accounts. John withdraws $80,000 per year, which pushes him into a higher tax bracket and triggers a larger Medicare premium. Lisa withdraws only $50,000 per year, staying in a lower bracket and saving thousands in taxes annually.

Planning how and when you withdraw, especially from different types of accounts, can make a big difference.

Mistake #4: Assuming it is too late to start

Some people believe that if they didn't start saving in their 20s or 30s, it's too late to make a difference. That's a common concern, but it's not the whole picture. You can't undo the past, but you can still make meaningful progress at any age.

Even saving for 10 to 15 years before retirement, with disciplined contributions and thoughtful investment choices, can provide meaningful support. And for those over age 50, catch-up contribution rules allow for higher annual savings, which can help accelerate progress later in the game.

Mistake #5: Making poor Social Security decisions

Social Security is a major source of retirement income, yet many people treat it like an afterthought. Some claim too early without fully understanding the long-term consequences. Others assume it will not be there at all and ignore it in their planning.

While the future of Social Security may involve some reforms, the program is unlikely to disappear. Making a informed claiming decision can mean the difference of tens or even hundreds of thousands of dollars over a lifetime.

Claiming too early or failing to coordinate benefits between spouses can place additional pressure on other retirement assets. Once a claiming decision is made, it can be difficult to undo, often requiring adjustments elsewhere in the retirement income plan..

Mistake #6: Underestimating healthcare and long-term care costs

People often assume expenses will decrease in retirement. While spending may drop during the mid-retirement years, it often climbs again in the later years due to increased healthcare needs.

Medical costs before Medicare eligibility can also be a major barrier to early retirement. Premiums under the Affordable Care Act can be substantial, particularly if income is too high to qualify for subsidies. This is where asset location can play an important role. If you have Roth assets to draw from, they will not count as taxable income and could help you qualify for reduced premiums.

Long-term care is another commonly overlooked cost. If one spouse becomes ill or requires in-home or facility care, it can place enormous financial strain on a couple's retirement assets. Too many families are caught off guard by this.

Crafting a retirement savings strategy isn't about finding a perfect formula or following a rigid set of rules. It's about understanding how different accounts work, how taxes show up over time, and how today's decisions can shape tomorrow's options.

When you take the time to think through where your savings are going, how they're taxed, and how flexible they'll be in the future, you're moving beyond autopilot. You're building a strategy that's intentional rather than accidental. That kind of clarity doesn't eliminate uncertainty, but it does give you more control over how you respond to it.

The goal of this chapter wasn't to tell you exactly what to do. It was to help you see the trade-offs, understand the consequences, and recognize where small adjustments can make a meaningful difference over time.

With a thoughtful savings structure in place, the next step is turning those savings into a plan that works for you in retirement. In the next chapter, we'll shift from accumulation to investing principles — focusing on how to grow your assets responsibly while managing risk, behavior, and expectations along the way.

References

1. Northwestern Mutual. "How Much Should I Have in My 401(k) by Age 60?"
   https://www.northwesternmutual.com/life-and-money/how-much-should-i-have-in-my-401k-by-age-60

2. Society for Human Resource Management (SHRM). "One in Four Workers Misses Full 401(k) Match."
   https://www.shrm.org/topics-tools/news/benefits-compensation/one-four-workers-miss-full-401k-match

CHAPTER 5
INVESTING LIKE AN ADVISOR— SMART, STRATEGIC, AND STRESS- FREE

Now that you have a strong savings strategy in place, it's time to turn your attention to investing. Many people believe investing is about picking hot stocks or timing the market just right. But that kind of thinking often leads to poor outcomes. An advisor-style approach does not rely on chasing returns or guessing what the market will do next. Instead, it emphasizes building disciplined, diversified portfolios that align with long-term goals and are adjusted intentionally as those goals evolve.

In this chapter, you'll be introduced to the core principles that shape a professional, long-term approach to investing. These aren't secret formulas or flashy trends. They are time-tested ideas that can help you avoid common mistakes, stay focused during market volatility, and get the most out of the money you've worked so hard to save.

You'll see why protecting your investments from large losses matters more than chasing every bit of upside, why diversification is more than just owning a handful of funds, and how staying invested through all market cycles often beats trying to predict the next big move. This chapter also explores how emotions affect performance, how to think critically about investment costs, and why the account you hold your investments in can be just as important as the investments themselves.

Each section is designed to help you build confidence in your investment decisions and understand how a long-term, advisor-style mindset can work in your favor.

THE PRINCIPLES OF INVESTING

Smart investing doesn't require a crystal ball. A disciplined, long-term investment approach is built around a handful of well-established principles. These are simple ideas that can make a meaningful difference over time. When applied consistently, they can help reduce guesswork and reduce emotionally driven decisions, even during periods of market volatility.

Rather than focusing on predictions or short-term results, this chapter introduces six core investing principles that shape how experienced investors approach risk, return, and long-term planning.

- **Don't lose money.** Large losses can be difficult to recover from, making risk management just as important as return potential.
- **Diversification matters.** Spreading investments across different assets can help reduce the impact of any single investment or market segment underperforming.
- **Time in the market often beats timing the market.** Staying invested through market cycles has historically been more effective than trying to predict short-term movements.
- **Manage your emotions.** Fear and greed can lead to decisions that work against long-term goals, especially during periods of volatility.
- **Costs matter.** Fees and expenses reduce net returns, and even small differences can compound meaningfully over time.

- **Asset location matters.** Where investments are held can influence taxes and after-tax outcomes, sometimes as much as the investments themselves.

These principles are not guarantees, and no investment strategy is risk-free. Losses are always possible. But understanding how these ideas fit together provides a strong foundation for more thoughtful investment decisions.

Each principle is explored in greater detail in the sections that follow.

PRINCIPLE 1: DON'T LOSE MONEY

One of the most fundamental investing principles is simple: don't lose money. That might sound obvious, but it's not just about avoiding losses altogether. It's about understanding the mindset behind managing risk, making thoughtful decisions during market downturns, and recognizing the difference between a temporary decline and a permanent mistake.

The challenge is that investors often want the best of both worlds. They pursue high returns while hoping to avoid any downside. Markets don't work that way. If you want the potential for meaningful growth, risk is unavoidable. The goal is not to eliminate risk, but to balance risk and reward in a way that aligns with your comfort level, time horizon, and long-term plan.

A big part of this mindset is understanding the real cost of large losses. The bigger the drop, the harder it is to recover.

Example:

If you invest $10,000 and lose 50 percent, your investment falls to $5,000. To return to $10,000, you now need a 100 percent gain, not another 50 percent. That kind of recovery takes time, patience, and often a favorable market environment. This is why managing downside risk matters. Recovering from modest declines is a normal part of investing.

Recovering from severe losses can take years and may disrupt a retirement plan if not anticipated.

It's also important to distinguish between temporary declines and realized losses. When an investment falls in value but you continue to hold it, you still own the same number of shares. The loss only becomes permanent when you sell. Selling in response to fear during a downturn can turn a short-term decline into a lasting setback.

An advisor-style way of thinking focuses on balance. Instead of reacting to market swings or trying to avoid losses entirely, the question becomes: how much growth is needed to meet long-term goals, and how much downside can be tolerated without abandoning the plan? That balance is central to managing risk effectively.

Risk can't be eliminated, and it shouldn't be ignored. But it should be understood. Diversification, for example, is one way to help manage downside exposure. Holding a mix of assets—such as stocks, bonds, real estate, and cash—can reduce the impact of any single investment or market segment underperforming. When one part of a portfolio struggles, another may provide stability.

Not losing money doesn't mean avoiding every decline or never seeing a lower account balance from one statement to the next. It means protecting long-term outcomes and staying aligned with a plan through inevitable market ups and downs. When you understand how losses affect your strategy and approach risk intentionally, you are beginning to think like an advisor.

PRINCIPLE 2: DIVERSIFICATION IS KEY

Diversification is one of the most misunderstood principles in investing. Many investors think they're diversified because they own several different stocks or a few mutual funds. But true diversification goes deeper. It's not just about how many holdings you have. It's about what those holdings are, how they behave in different environments, and how they work together in a portfolio.

At its core, diversification means not putting all your eggs in one basket. By spreading investments across different asset classes, sectors, and types of investments, the impact of any single downturn can be reduced. Diversification helps manage risk. It doesn't eliminate the possibility of loss, but it can soften the impact and make periods of volatility easier to navigate.

That said, there's a tradeoff. A well-diversified portfolio is likely to have a lower expected return than a single high-growth asset like the S&P 500. That's by design. If you build a portfolio that includes stocks, bonds, and cash, it won't match the highs of an all-stock index in a bull market, but it also may not experience the same depth of losses during a bear market. That's why comparing a diversified portfolio to a pure equity benchmark can be unfair. A blended benchmark that reflects the actual mix of your investments provides a more accurate comparison.

Some investors think that owning four or five different individual stocks makes them diversified. In reality, those stocks often move in the same direction, especially if they belong to the same sector or are highly correlated. If all holdings rise and fall together, your risk hasn't been reduced, it has simply been disguised. Effective diversification looks beyond the number of positions and focuses on how those positions behave relative to each other.

A simple example illustrates this difference.

John puts all his money into a single stock, Example Company XYZ. It performs well for a while, but then the company runs into trouble and the stock tanks. John loses a big chunk of his portfolio.

Lisa, on the other hand, spreads her money across different stocks, bonds, and real estate. When one investment underperforms, the others help offset the impact. Her portfolio doesn't avoid losses entirely, but they tend to be less severe and recovery is often faster.

Different types of assets behave differently in different markets:

- Stocks offer the highest growth potential but also tend to experience the most volatility

- Bonds generally provide more stable income and often hold up better when stocks struggle
- Real estate can offer diversification beyond traditional markets and may help protect against inflation
- Cash or short-term investments provide stability and liquidity when it is needed most

No single asset class consistently performs best year after year. Diversification reduces the need to guess which investment will outperform next. Instead, a diversified portfolio can remain aligned with long-term goals even when certain components underperform for extended periods.

Diversification isn't about eliminating risk. It's about spreading risk in a thoughtful, intentional way that aligns with personal goals and risk tolerance. While it won't prevent losses, it can help reduce their severity and make the emotional side of investing easier to manage. When done well, it can keep you in the game—and sometimes that discipline matters more than any single return.

Are You Really Diversified?

Many investors assume their portfolios are well diversified, but a closer look often reveals gaps they may not have realized. Portfolios that appear varied on the surface can still be more concentrated than intended. It is easy to mistake variety for true diversification without examining asset classes, sectors, correlation, and overlap more closely.

One clear illustration of why diversification matters is the Callan Periodic Table of Investment Returns. This chart ranks asset classes by performance each year. The results show how unpredictable markets can be—asset classes that lead one year may fall to the bottom the next. No single category dominates consistently, and the frequent reshuffling highlights the danger of chasing past performance. A diversified portfolio helps smooth this volatility by spreading exposure across multiple asset types [1]. The full chart can be found in Appendix A for reference.

Consider a common scenario: an investor owns one mutual fund or ETF along with five individual stocks. At first glance, this may seem like a reasonable mix. A closer evaluation begins with the allocation. Does the fund or ETF represent 80 percent of the portfolio, with the individual stocks making up the remainder? Or is the balance reversed? The weighting of each holding can dramatically change the risk profile.

Next, the fund itself matters. Is it primarily invested in stocks, bonds, or a blend of asset classes? A fund concentrated in growth stocks will behave very differently from a conservative bond fund or a balanced fund with broader exposure.

The individual stocks also deserve closer inspection. What sectors do they represent? How much of the total portfolio does each stock account for? Are there overlaps between the fund holdings and the individual stocks? Do the stocks tend to move together, indicating high correlation? Holdings that rise and fall in tandem provide less diversification than their number alone might suggest.

Even if the five stocks come from five different sectors, that still represents exposure to fewer than half of the eleven sectors in the S&P 500—and only one company per sector. Could that still be diversified? Possibly, but it depends on position size, weighting, and how the fund is invested. Without that information, it is impossible to draw a meaningful conclusion.

A diversified portfolio does not assure a profit or protect against loss in a declining market. Asset allocation is an investment strategy that will not guarantee a profit or protect you from loss. Asset allocation, which is driven by complex mathematical models, should not be confused with the much simpler concept of diversification.

Another common example involves 401(k) participants who own four or five mutual funds from their plan menu. Different fund names do not always mean different exposures. Many of these funds may rely on the same group of large-cap U.S. stocks, reducing diversification through overlap and correlation.

And this is more common than many investors realize. According to multiple large studies, the average 401(k) participant has between 70 and 75 percent of their portfolio allocated to equities, including target-date funds [2][3][4][5]. While that level of equity exposure may be appropriate for younger investors, it can be too aggressive for those in their 50s or 60s.

One of the biggest issues is a behavioral pattern known as "target-date plus one." This happens when participants invest in a target-date fund and then add another equity fund on top, often duplicating the same holdings and increasing overall risk without realizing it [2][6]. Another common issue is the "1/n strategy," where contributions are split evenly across the available fund menu. When plan menus are equity-heavy, so is the resulting portfolio [6][7].

Company stock adds another layer of concentration risk. Despite the risks of single-stock exposure, many 401(k) plans still have 4 to 9 percent of participant assets concentrated in employer shares [2][3][4]. This creates added vulnerability, particularly if a company experiences financial trouble and both employment income and retirement savings are affected at the same time.

So how can diversification be evaluated in a meaningful way?

In some cases, recognizing familiar mutual funds or ETFs can provide a general sense of a portfolio's focus. However, that kind of surface-level assessment is rarely enough. A more accurate picture comes from examining how individual holdings are weighted and how they interact with one another. This often involves reviewing fund composition, sector exposure, correlation, and overlap across the entire portfolio.

Portfolio analysis tools can help provide this clarity. One example is a Morningstar Snapshot report, which highlights how investments are distributed across asset classes and sectors, and how closely holdings move together. These kinds of tools are designed to look beyond names and labels to reveal how diversified a portfolio truly is.

A portfolio may appear diversified at a glance, but real diversification requires understanding what is owned, how those holdings fit together, and how the portfolio is likely to behave as market conditions change.

PRINCIPLE 3: TIME IN THE MARKET BEATS TIMING THE MARKET

One of the most persistent myths in investing is that returns can be improved by jumping in and out of the market at just the right times. History and data tell a different story.

Consistent, long-term investing almost always outperforms attempts to predict the market's highs and lows. Trying to time the market often leads to worse outcomes than simply staying invested. Some of the market's biggest gains tend to come shortly after its steepest declines, making it nearly impossible to know when to be in or out. Missing just a few of the best days can have a devastating impact on long-term performance.

Between January 2004 and December 2023, an investor who stayed fully invested in the S&P 500 earned an average annual return of 9.8 percent. If that same investor missed just the 10 best days in the market, their annual return dropped to 5.6 percent. Missing the best 20 days reduced the return to 3.3 percent annually, and missing the 30 best days cut it further to just 1.2 percent per year [8].

This pattern is not unusual. Over the last 30 years, similar data shows that missing the best 10 to 30 days in the market consistently erodes long-term performance [9]. What is more, these best days often occur during periods of extreme volatility, sometimes within days of the worst-performing sessions. That makes them nearly impossible to predict.

In addition to timing mistakes, behavioral factors often get in the way. The average investor tends to underperform the very funds they are invested in, not because the funds did poorly, but because investors bought high, sold low, and chased performance.

Morningstar's *Mind the Gap 2024* report is an example of this. It found that, over the 10-year period ending in 2023, investors earned about 15 percent less than the total returns generated by the mutual funds they were invested in. While the average fund delivered an annualized return of 7.3 percent, the average investor only captured 6.2 percent. The gap was widest in more volatile fund categories, where attempts to time the market were most damaging [10].

Other long-running research supports this pattern. Dalbar's *Quantitative Analysis of Investor Behavior* has shown for decades that average investors routinely underperform both the market and the funds they invest in because of poor timing and emotionally driven decision-making [11].

One antidote to this behavior is dollar-cost averaging: making consistent contributions at regular intervals, regardless of market conditions. This strategy removes emotion from the decision-making process. By continuing to buy through market ups and downs, investors naturally purchase more shares when prices are low and fewer when they are high. It encourages steady participation, which is the foundation of long-term success.

While portfolios may be adjusted over time to reflect changing goals or risk tolerance, attempting to avoid volatility by exiting and re-entering the market has historically proven difficult. A broad body of research shows that even relatively short periods out of the market can make a meaningful difference over time.

For example, during the early stages of COVID-19 in 2020, the market dropped sharply in March but rebounded in the months that followed. Many investors panicked, exited the market, and waited for conditions to "calm down." Some never re-entered. Those who remained invested participated in the subsequent recovery, which many market observers describe as a V-shaped rebound [12]. The recovery was not linear, and the timing of re-entry proved difficult for many investors.

The truth is, there will almost always be reasons to feel uneasy about the market. Economic headlines, elections, and global events cannot be predicted with accuracy or consistency. Rather than trying to forecast the future, the focus is on staying invested in a strategy that matches long-term goals and risk tolerance, even during periods of uncertainty.

The best time to invest is when you have money to invest. The best way to stay invested is to build a plan that accounts for volatility and stick to it. Time in the market beats timing the market, not just in theory, but in real returns, real behavior, and real outcomes. *Stick to the plan!*

Historical data is not indicative of future results. Market conditions can change. Past performance does not guarantee future results. Dollar cost averaging will not guarantee a profit or protect you from loss, but may reduce your average cost per share in a fluctuating market.

PRINCIPLE 4: MANAGE YOUR EMOTIONS

Investing is not just about math and markets. It is also about mindset. Emotional decisions often lead to poor investment outcomes. Many investors underperform not because of the investments themselves, but because of how they react to market changes. Fear and greed are powerful forces, and they often drive investors to buy high, sell low, and abandon long-term strategies at exactly the wrong times.

This behavior is not just anecdotal. It has been studied and documented for years. One of the clearest findings in behavioral finance is that emotional decisions tend to reduce returns over time. The cycle is familiar: investors get excited during strong markets and increase exposure after gains have already occurred. Then, when markets fall, fear takes over and investments are sold, locking in losses. The result is performance chasing rather than disciplined wealth building.

Several well-documented behavioral biases help explain this pattern:
- **Loss aversion**: The pain of losing money feels greater than the satisfaction of gains, often leading to irrational decisions
- **Overconfidence**: Believing you can consistently predict what markets will do can result in excessive trading and risk-taking
- **Recency bias**: Overweighting recent events can cause investors to believe short-term patterns will continue

- **Herd behavior**: Following the crowd can lead to buying when prices are high and selling when prices are low
- **Anchoring**: Fixating on a particular price point, like what you paid for an investment, can distort rational decision-making

In his article *Common Investor Behaviors That Hurt Investments*, Wade Pfau explains how these tendencies can erode long-term results. He highlights that behavioral coaching—simply helping investors avoid harmful decisions—can add meaningful value over time. In fact, studies show that professional guidance can lead to better results, not because of superior stock picking, but because can reduce the odds of costly, emotional driven mistakes [13].

One study cited by Pfau found that retirement plan participants who received professional investment help earned an average of 3.32 percent more per year than those who managed on their own, even after accounting for fees [14].

A broader perspective can also influence behavior. Exposure to repeated market cycles and a wide range of investor reactions can help reveal patterns that are difficult to recognize from a single account or short time frame. Access to research, peer discussion, and long-term historical context can make it easier to filter short-term noise and maintain focus on long-term objectives.

Investors often say they will wait until the market "calms down" before investing again, but that moment rarely arrives. Uncertainty is a constant feature of financial markets. What separates more successful investors from less successful ones is not perfect timing or flawless allocation. It is the ability to remain disciplined when emotions are running high.

Staying the Course

Maintaining a disciplined investment approach involves reinforcing behaviors that support long-term consistency:

- **Set clear goals**: Define objectives and risk tolerance from the start
- **Diversify**: Spread investments across asset classes to reduce concentration risk
- **Rebalance periodically**: Adjust allocations to stay aligned with the original plan
- **Stick to the plan**: Avoid making changes based on short-term market movements
- **Keep investing**: Continue regular contributions, even during market downturns.
- **Review, don't react**: Revisit the plan when markets shift, rather than responding emotionally

Managing emotions does not eliminate risk or volatility. But it can significantly reduce the likelihood of costly mistakes. By staying focused on long-term goals and maintaining discipline through market cycles, investors improve the odds of more consistent decision-making over time.

Rebalancing may be a taxable event. Before you take any specific action be sure to consult with your tax professional.

PRINCIPLE 5: COSTS MATTER

Cost is one of the few variables investors can control. Every dollar paid in fees is a dollar that does not remain invested. Over time, those costs can compound and meaningfully affect results. That said, the lowest-cost investment is not always the best option. There is an important difference between cost and value, and thoughtful investors understand how to weigh one against the other.

In recent years, the investment industry has moved aggressively toward ultra-low-cost products. Index funds with expense ratios below 0.10 percent are now widely available. This shift has led many investors to assume that any fund with a higher expense ratio is automatically inferior. That assumption overlooks a more important question: what value is being delivered in exchange for the cost?

Higher costs can certainly hurt performance. But some actively managed funds have demonstrated consistent results, provided access to specialized segments of the market, or offered better risk control than comparable index funds. There are many examples of high-cost funds that underperform. There are also actively managed funds with moderate costs that have kept pace with, or even exceeded, relevant benchmarks over time.

Cost is an important factor when evaluating an investment, but it should not be the only one. A value-focused approach looks beyond fees to consider how consistently a fund follows its stated strategy, how disciplined the management team is, and whether the investment continues to serve its intended role within a portfolio.

For example, if a fund identifies as a mid-cap stock fund, it should remain focused on mid-cap stocks. When managers drift into large-cap or small-cap stocks in an effort to chase performance, the fund is no longer doing what it was selected to do. This kind of style drift can introduce unintended risk at the portfolio level by altering how the investment interacts with other holdings. Evaluating whether a fund behaves as intended is just as important as evaluating what it costs.

There is also a behavioral component to consider. Low-cost investing may work well in theory, but discipline is often harder to maintain in practice. Market volatility can cause even well-constructed portfolios to be abandoned at inopportune times. For many investors, having structure, perspective, and accountability can help reduce emotionally driven decisions that undermine long-term outcomes. In this context, the value of guidance often comes from helping investors stay consistent rather than from attempting to outperform the market.

Several tools are available to help evaluate investment costs:
- **Morningstar** provides detailed information on fund expenses, performance, and strategy
- **FINRA's Fund Analyzer** lets investors compare costs and estimate long-term impacts [15]

- **Fund fact sheets** are available from most investment companies and show basic expense data

A value-oriented mindset does not chase the cheapest option. It looks for the most appropriate fit. That includes evaluating performance, discipline, consistency, and the role an investment plays within a broader strategy.

Fees matter. But they are not everything. A low-cost fund can still be a poor fit, just as a moderately priced fund can sometimes deliver exactly what is needed. The goal is not simply to minimize costs, but to ensure that every dollar invested is working efficiently in support of long-term goals.

PRINCIPLE 6: ASSET LOCATION – WHERE YOU HOLD INVESTMENTS MATTERS

Investing is not just about selecting the right assets; it is also about placing those assets in the right types of accounts to maximize after-tax returns. This concept, known as asset location, focuses on the strategic placement of investments across taxable, tax-deferred, and tax-exempt accounts to enhance tax efficiency.

Understanding Asset Location

Asset location complements asset allocation. While asset allocation determines the mix of investments (stocks, bonds, etc.) based on risk tolerance and goals, asset location focuses on where to hold these investments to manage taxes. Different account types have varying tax treatments:

- **Taxable accounts**: Investments may be subject to capital gains taxes and taxes on dividends and interest income.
- **Tax-deferred accounts** (such as Traditional IRAs or 401(k)s): Taxes are deferred until withdrawals are made, at which point income is generally taxed at ordinary income rates.

- **Tax-exempt accounts** (such as Roth IRAs): Contributions are made with after-tax dollars, but qualified withdrawals are tax-free.

Strategic Placement of Assets

From an asset location perspective, certain investment types tend to be more tax-efficient in specific accounts:

- **Hold tax-efficient investments** such as index funds, ETFs, or growth-oriented stocks are often held in taxable accounts, where lower turnover and long-term capital gains treatment may reduce ongoing tax impact
- **Hold tax-inefficient investments** such as bonds, REITs, or actively managed mutual funds with high turnover, are often better suited for tax-deferred or tax-exempt accounts where annual income and short-term gains are not immediately taxed

For example, interest income generated by bonds held in a taxable account is typically taxed at ordinary income rates. Holding those same bonds inside a tax-deferred account, such as a traditional IRA or 401(k), allows taxes to be deferred until withdrawals begin, potentially at a lower tax rate in retirement. Meanwhile, placing index funds or ETFs in a taxable brokerage account may allow investors to benefit from long-term capital gains treatment. In some cases, market declines may also create opportunities for tax-loss harvesting, a concept introduced earlier in Chapter 4 as part of long-term planning.

IMPACT ON AFTER-TAX RETURNS

Asset location can have a meaningful impact over time. Research from Charles Schwab suggests that proper asset placement can increase after-tax returns by approximately 0.14% to 0.41% annually for conservative investors in mid- to high-income tax brackets. For a retired couple with a $2 million portfolio, this improvement could translate into a reduction in tax drag of roughly $2,800 to $8,200 per year, depending on individual circumstances [16].

For a comprehensive review of your personal situation, always consult with a tax or legal advisor. Neither Cetera Wealth Services LLC nor any of its representatives may give legal or tax advice.

PUTTING IT ALL TOGETHER

Asset location is still a relatively new concept to many individual investors, but it has the potential to improve long-term outcomes. Understanding how different types of income are taxed and how that taxation varies by account type, can help reduce the drag taxes place on a portfolio. This does not require a complete overhaul.. This does not require overhauling everything. Even small adjustments, such as holding certain investments in more tax-appropriate accounts, can add up over time. The key is being intentional about both what is invested and where those investments are held.

WRAPPING UP: INVEST LIKE AN ADVISOR

Smart investing is not about luck or perfect timing. It is about following clear principles, staying focused on long-term goals, and making decisions based on strategy rather than emotion. Structure, discipline, and perspective play an important role in navigating uncertainty.

By adopting principles such as protecting against large losses, diversifying wisely, staying invested, managing emotions, weighing costs carefully, and being intentional about where investments are held, it becomes possible to build a strategy designed to support long-term outcomes.

Keep learning, stay steady, and remember that investing is a marathon, not a sprint.

References

1. Callan LLC. *The Callan Periodic Table of Investment Returns (2005–2024)*. https://www.callan.com/periodic-table/

2. The Vanguard Group. *How America Saves 2024: An Analysis of 2023 Defined-Contribution Plan Data.* June 2024.

3. T. Rowe Price Retirement Plan Services. *Reference Point 2024: 2023 401(k) Benchmarking Report.* 2024.

4. Alight Solutions. *Alight Solutions 401(k) Index™: 2024 Observations.* January 2025.

5. Holden S, Bass S, Copeland C. "401(k) Plan Asset Allocation, Account Balances, and Loan Activity in 2022." *EBRI Issue Brief* No. 606. April 2024.

6. Benartzi S, Thaler RH. "Naive Diversification Strategies in Defined Contribution Saving Plans." *American Economic Review.* 2001; 91(1): 79–98.

7. Huberman G, Jiang W. "Offering versus Choice in 401(k) Plans: Equity Exposure and Number of Funds." *Journal of Finance.* 2006; 61(2): 763–801.

8. Fool Wealth. *The Cost of Missing the Market's Best Days.* https://foolwealth.com/hubfs/one-pager/timing-the-market.pdf

9. Wells Fargo Advisors. *Investing in Volatile Markets: The Cost of Missing the Best Days.* https://www.wellsfargoadvisors.com/research-analysis/reports/policy/volatile-markets.htm

10. Morningstar Portfolio & Planning Research. *Mind the Gap 2024: Investors lost out on about 15% of the return their funds generated.* August 15, 2024. https://assets.contentstack.io/v3/assets/blt4eb669caa7dc65b2/blt0

571178b63219c0b/66bdeb4a4f0e4749e15a5621/2024_Mind_the
_Gap.pdf

11. Dalbar, Inc. *Quantitative Analysis of Investor Behavior (QAIB),
    2021 Edition.* https://www.dalbar.com/QAIB

12. Morningstar. *Coronavirus Market Crash Was the Shortest Bear
    Market in History.*
    https://www.morningstar.com/portfolios/long-history-market-
    crashes-coronavirus-crash-was-shortest

13. Pfau, W. *Common Investor Behaviors That Hurt
    Investments.* Retirement Researcher.
    https://retirementresearcher.com/common-investor-
    behaviors-hurt-investments/

14. Financial Engines and Aon Hewitt. *Help in Defined Contribution
    Plans: 2006 Through 2012. https://aon.mediaroom.com/news-
    releases?item=136959#:~:text=A%20new%20study%20from%2
    0Financial,%2DHelp%20participant%20($32%2C800).*

15. FINRA. *Fund Analyzer.* https://tools.finra.org/fund_analyzer/

16. Charles Schwab. *How Asset Location Can Help Save on Taxes.*
    https://www.schwab.com/learn/story/how-asset-location-can-
    help-save-on-taxes

CHAPTER 6
MASTERING SOCIAL SECURITY AND
MEDICARE STRATEGIES

Retirement planning is more than just saving and investing. Two of the most important programs that support Americans in retirement, Social Security and Medicare, are also among the most misunderstood. Confusion about when to claim benefits or what Medicare actually covers can lead to costly decisions. Too often, choices are made based on outdated advice, common myths, or what happened to work for someone else.

This chapter takes a practical look at both programs. It explains how Social Security benefits are calculated, how claiming decisions affect monthly income, and why coordinating benefits within a household can make a meaningful difference. It also addresses persistent myths, including concerns about whether the program will be around in the future or whether funds have been misused.

The second half of the chapter focuses on Medicare, another essential but often confusing part of retirement planning. It provides a high-level overview of what Parts A, B, C, and D cover, what they cost, and where coverage gaps can create unexpected expenses. The discussion also introduces the Income-Related Monthly Adjustment Amount (IRMAA), a lesser-known cost that can surprise higher-income retirees, and explains why understanding how the system works is critical before making decisions.

This chapter is not designed to make you an expert in either program. Instead, the goal is to help you think more like an advisor by understanding how Social Security and Medicare function and how they fit into a well-designed retirement income strategy.

UNDERSTANDING SOCIAL SECURITY: MORE THAN JUST A CHECK

Social Security is more than just a monthly deposit. It is a foundational piece of retirement income planning that provides inflation-adjusted, government-backed payments for life. Yet many people misunderstand how the program works or underestimate the impact their claiming decisions can have on long-term financial security.

This section explains how benefits are determined, addresses common misconceptions, and explores how claiming decisions can make a substantial difference in retirement outcomes.

THE BIGGEST MYTHS ABOUT SOCIAL SECURITY

Before exploring how Social Security works, it helps to clear up several widespread misconceptions that often lead to poor decisions.

- **"Social Security won't be there for me."** This myth overlooks the program's dedicated funding and legal structure. Even without legislative reform, Social Security is projected to continue paying the majority of scheduled benefits for decades.
- **"The government stole the money."** Social Security Trust Funds are invested in interest-bearing U.S. Treasury bonds. The funds have been used as intended under the law and continue to earn interest backed by the U.S. government.
- **"Claim early so you don't miss out."** This is often one of the least efficient ways to claim. It can reduce your lifetime income and, for married couples, weaken potential survivor benefits.
- **"Planning doesn't matter."** Decisions about when to claim, how benefits are coordinated between spouses, and how Social Security interacts with taxes and Medicare can have a meaningful impact on retirement outcomes.

HOW SOCIAL SECURITY BENEFITS ARE CALCULATED

Your Social Security benefit is based on your highest 35 years of earnings, indexed for inflation. These earnings are used to calculate your average indexed monthly earnings (AIME). If you have fewer than 35 years of earnings (such as a someone who spent time out of the workforce), zeros are factored in, which reduces your average.

Once your AIME is calculated, it is applied to a three-tier formula to determine your Primary Insurance Amount (PIA), which is the monthly benefit you receive at full retirement age. For those turning 62 in 2025, the formula is:

- 90% of the first $1,226 of AIME
- 32% of the amount between $1,226 and $7,391
- 15% of the amount above $7,391 [1]

Example: High Earner With Maximum Wages

Suppose someone earned the maximum taxable Social Security wage base ($170,100 in 2025) every year for 35 years. Their AIME would be $13,689.

Using the 2025 bend points:
- 90% of $1,226 = $1,103.40
- 32% of $6,165 = $1,972.80
- 15% of $6,298 = $944.70

PIA = $4,020.90 per month at full retirement age

This monthly benefit forms the baseline. Cost-of-living adjustments (COLAs) are added annually, helping preserve purchasing power in retirement.

BEFORE YOU CLAIM: THINK BIGGER

Many people ask the same question when they approach retirement: "Should I just take Social Security as soon as I can?" It's a fair question. After contributing to the system for decades, the idea of starting benefits as early as possible can feel urgent, especially amid uncertainty about the future.

But making a claiming decision without considering the broader picture can have long-term consequences. Social Security is one of the few income sources designed to last for life and adjust for inflation. For married couples, the decision also affects potential survivor benefits. Focusing only on when benefits can begin often overlooks how those benefits fit into an overall retirement income strategy.

There is no single right answer for everyone. Factors such as longevity expectations, tax considerations, spousal benefits, and other income sources all play a role. Asking a broader question—how Social Security fits into the rest of a retirement plan—can lead to more informed and effective decisions over time.

FINDING YOUR OWN SOCIAL SECURITY BENEFIT INFORMATION

Before making any decisions about when or how to claim benefits, it is important to know where you stand. The best way to do that is by creating a mySocialSecurity account at www.ssa.gov/myaccount. This secure online portal allows you to view your earnings history, check your estimated future benefits, and confirm your eligibility for different types of benefits.

Reviewing your record regularly can also help catch any errors in your reported earnings, which could affect your future payments. It is a simple step that gives you access to the information you need to start making informed decisions.

CLAIMING EARLY, ON TIME, OR LATER

You can claim Social Security as early as age 62, but doing so permanently reduces your monthly benefit. Claiming before full retirement age results in a reduction of about 5 to 6 percent per year. On the other hand, delaying benefits past full retirement age results in a permanent increase of 8 percent more for each year delayed, up to age 70 [2].

Let's say your full retirement benefit (PIA) is $3,849 per month and your full retirement age is 67:

- Claiming at 62: $2,697 per month (70% of PIA)
- Claiming at 67: $3,849 per month (100% of PIA)
- Claiming at 70: $4,777 per month (124% of PIA)

These amounts do not include Medicare premium deductions or taxation, which can reduce your actual deposit.

UNDERSTANDING THE ANNUAL EARNINGS TEST

If you claim benefits before full retirement age and continue to work, some of your benefits may be withheld. This is known as the earnings test. In 2025, $1 in benefits is withheld for every $2 earned above $23,400. In the year you reach full retirement age, the limit increases, and only $1 is withheld for every $3 earned above $62,400 [3].

Once you reach full retirement age, the test no longer applies. Benefits that were withheld are effectively returned through recalculated payments.

SPOUSAL, SURVIVOR, AND DIVORCED BENEFITS

Social Security offers benefits not just to workers, but also to spouses, survivors, and some divorced individuals.

- **Spousal Benefits**: A non-working or lower-earning spouse can claim up to 50 percent of the higher-earning spouse's PIA, provided the higher-earning spouse has already claimed [4].
- **Survivor Benefits**: If a spouse passes away, the surviving spouse can receive the higher of their own benefit or their deceased spouse's benefit. Survivor benefits can be claimed as early as age 60, but benefits are reduced if claimed before full retirement age.
- **Divorced Spouse Benefits**: If you were married at least 10 years, are currently unmarried, your ex-spouse is at least age 62 may be eligible to claim spousal or survivor benefits based on an ex-spouse's earnings record, provided the divorce occurred more than two years ago.

These benefit options add complexity to Social Security planning. Coordinating spousal and survivor benefits can meaningfully affect lifetime income and should be evaluated as part of a broader retirement income framework.

TAXES AND MEDICARE PREMIUMS

Many people are surprised to learn that Social Security is taxable. Depending on your provisional income, which includes your adjusted gross income, tax-free interest, and half your Social Security benefits, up to 85 percent of your benefit may be subject to federal income tax [5].

In addition, Medicare Part B premiums are usually deducted directly from your monthly benefit. These premiums increase if your income exceeds certain thresholds. Understanding how Social Security interacts with both taxes and Medicare is essential for accurate retirement income planning.

WHY TIMING MATTERS

Many people claim benefits at 62 simply because they can, or because they worry the program may not be there in the future. In some cases, this may not result in the best outcome.

Decisions about when to claim benefits are often influenced by several factors, including health, expected longevity, income needs, taxes, and the potential impact on a spouse's benefits. For individuals who expect to live longer or whose spouse may rely on survivor benefits, delaying Social Security can meaningfully increase total lifetime income.

Social Security also plays a critical role in retirement income planning. A higher guaranteed benefit can reduce the pressure on investment withdrawals, helping manage market risk and sequence-of-returns risk. When viewed as part of a broader income strategy, delaying benefits may improve both retirement security and tax efficiency.

This information may not be relied on for the purpose of determining your social security benefits or eligibility, or avoiding any federal tax penalties. You are encouraged to seek advice from your own tax or legal professional.

UNDERSTANDING MEDICARE: WHAT IT COVERS, AND WHAT IT DOESN'T

Medicare is a critical part of retirement health care planning, but it is also one of the most misunderstood. Many people assume that once they qualify for Medicare, all of their medical expenses will be covered. That is not the case. Medicare provides a solid foundation, but it leaves several important gaps in coverage, which can come as a surprise to retirees who are not prepared.

What Medicare Covers

Medicare is divided into four parts, each serving a different role in your health care coverage:

- **Part A** covers inpatient hospital care, skilled nursing facility care, hospice, and some home health care. Most people do not pay a premium for Part A, but there are deductibles and coinsurance costs.
- **Part B** covers doctor visits, outpatient care, preventive services, and some home health care. In 2025, the standard Part B premium is $185 per month [6].
- **Part C**, also known as Medicare Advantage, is an alternative to Original Medicare. These are private insurance plans approved by Medicare that often include additional benefits such as vision, dental, or prescription drug coverage. Costs and coverage vary widely by plan and by location.
- **Part D** covers prescription drugs. This coverage is optional but important, and it requires choosing a separate plan or selecting a Medicare Advantage plan that includes drug benefits.

WHAT MEDIGAP PLANS DO

For those enrolled in Original Medicare (Parts A and B), a **Medigap** policy can help fill in the coverage gaps. These are standardized supplemental insurance plans sold by private companies to help pay for out-of-pocket costs that Medicare does not fully cover, such as copayments, coinsurance, and deductibles. Medigap policies do not replace Medicare, but instead work alongside it to reduce your share of covered medical expenses. Importantly, Medigap policies do not include coverage for dental, vision, hearing aids, or long-term care. Individuals who want those services need to seek separate coverage. Choosing the right Medigap plan can make your health care costs more predictable in retirement and help protect against unexpected medical bills. It is important to note that individuals cannot have a Medigap plan and a Medicare Advantage plan at the same time.

THE INCOME-RELATED MONTHLY ADJUSTMENT AMOUNT (IRMAA)

Many people are surprised to learn that Medicare premiums are not the same for everyone. If your income is above a certain level, you will pay more for both Part B and Part D. This additional cost is known as the Income-Related Monthly Adjustment Amount (IRMAA), and it is based on your modified adjusted gross income (MAGI) from two years earlier.

In 2025, individuals with MAGI over $106,000, or married couples filing jointly with MAGI over $212,000, will begin paying IRMAA. These charges are applied in tiers and the tiers are adjusted each year [8].

Understanding how income affects your Medicare premiums is essential. Actions like Roth conversions, required minimum distributions, or capital gains can push you into a higher IRMAA bracket. These additional costs can have a meaningful impact on your retirement budget if not properly planned for.

THE BIGGEST MYTH ABOUT MEDICARE

A common misconception is that Medicare covers all your health care needs. While it does provide broad protection, retirees often face significant out-of-pocket expenses. In fact, a healthy 65-year-old couple retiring today may need over $300,000 to cover health care costs throughout retirement, even with Medicare [7].

Failing to understand these gaps can lead to sticker shock when the first medical bills arrive. Planning ahead and selecting appropriate supplemental coverage can help manage these risks.

WHY YOU SHOULDN'T GO IT ALONE

Medicare coverage decisions are rarely simple. The number of available options, frequent rule changes, and regional differences in plan availability can make the process overwhelming. Missing enrollment deadlines or selecting an inappropriate plan can lead to higher costs, coverage gaps, or penalties that are difficult to reverse.

Because of this complexity, it is often helpful to involve a knowledgeable, trusted resource when evaluating Medicare choices. That may include a licensed Medicare advisor, a local SHIP counselor (State Health Insurance Assistance Program), or a financial planner who understands how Medicare fits within a broader retirement strategy.

Seeking guidance does not mean giving up control. It means making decisions based on accurate, up-to-date information rather than assumptions or incomplete understanding. When it comes to Medicare, the cost of a misstep can be significant, and taking the time to get informed support can help reduce unnecessary risk.

Understanding how Social Security and Medicare work provides an essential foundation, but these programs are only part of a broader financial picture. They interact with investment strategies, tax planning, and withdrawal decisions in ways that can meaningfully affect long-term outcomes. In the next chapter, we will shift from understanding individual systems to exploring more advanced strategies for building and managing wealth, with a focus on how these pieces work together over time.

References

1. Social Security Administration. "Bend Points for 2025." https://www.ssa.gov/oact/cola/bendpoints.html

2. Social Security Administration. "Retirement Benefits." SSA Publication No. 05-10035. https://www.ssa.gov/pubs/EN-05-10035.pdf

3. Social Security Administration. "How Work Affects Your Benefits." SSA Publication No. 05-10069. https://www.ssa.gov/pubs/EN-05-10069.pdf

4. Social Security Administration. "What Every Woman Should Know." SSA Publication No. 05-10127. https://www.ssa.gov/pubs/EN-05-10127.pdf

5. Social Security Administration. "Retirement Benefits." SSA Publication No. 05-10035. https://www.ssa.gov/pubs/EN-05-10035.pdf

6. Medicare.gov. "Part A and Part B Costs for 2025." https://www.medicare.gov/basics/costs/medicare-costs

7. **Kiplinger.** *Guide to Planning for Health Care Costs in Retirement.* Kiplinger, June 2024. https://www.kiplinger.com/kiplinger-advisor-collective/planning-for-health-care-costs-in-retirement

8. Kiplinger. "Medicare Premiums 2025: IRMAA for Parts B and D." https://www.kiplinger.com/retirement/medicare/medicare-premiums-2025-irmaa-for-parts-b-and-d

CHAPTER 7
ADVANCED STRATEGIES FOR BUILDING AND MANAGING WEALTH

By now, you've built a solid foundation for retirement. You've taken inventory of your financial life, learned how to save strategically, and explored how Social Security and Medicare fit into the picture. The next step is understanding how all of these pieces come together to create a reliable, tax-smart income strategy.

Retirement income planning is not just about pulling money from an account when needed. The order in which you withdraw from different accounts can have lasting effects on taxes and portfolio longevity. Many people are surprised to learn how much more efficient a plan can become with just a few well-timed, intentional decisions.

This chapter explores three areas that play an important role in long-term success. First, it looks at tax-efficient withdrawal strategies, including how to evaluate Roth conversions and time Qualified Charitable Distributions. Next, it examines common retirement income sources and how they are often layered to balance stability, flexibility, and risk. Finally, it introduces a range of alternative investments that are frequently misunderstood but may be appropriate for certain investors under specific circumstances.

The goal is to provide a clear understanding of the tools available, the tradeoffs involved, and how these strategies can work together. In the next chapter, this foundation will be used to show how a retirement paycheck can be constructed and sustained over time.

TAX-EFFICIENT WITHDRAWAL STRATEGIES: MAKING YOUR MONEY LAST LONGER

Once you reach retirement, the question shifts from "How much do I have saved?" to "How do I use this money without giving too much away in taxes?" The order in which you take money from your accounts matters more than people realize. A structured withdrawal strategy often follows a deliberate order that builds on the same tax-aware thinking used during the accumulation phase, including asset location. Just as holding the right investments in the right account types can reduce tax drag while you are saving, coordinating withdrawals across taxable, tax-deferred, and Roth accounts can minimize taxes and help your savings last longer in retirement.

THE CONVENTIONAL WITHDRAWAL ORDER

In a typical retirement withdrawal strategy, the order in which income is drawn is often considered as follows:

1. **Taxable accounts first**
   These include brokerage accounts where you have already paid taxes on the money you invested. Withdrawals here often generate capital gains, dividends, or interest income, which are usually taxed at lower rates than traditional retirement income.

2. **Tax-deferred accounts second**
   Traditional IRAs, 401(k)s and similar accounts grow tax-deferred, but distributions are taxed as ordinary income. Delaying withdrawals helps these accounts grow, but required minimum distributions (RMDs) will eventually force withdrawals, starting at age 73 for most retirees.

3. **Roth accounts last**
   Roth IRAs and Roth 401(k)s grow tax-free and can be withdrawn tax-free in retirement. Holding these until later years helps preserve tax-advantaged dollars for higher tax environments or legacy planning.

This order aims to lower your lifetime tax liability and avoid jumping into higher tax brackets earlier than necessary. However, it is not always as simple as following a single sequence. In some cases, blending withdrawals from multiple account types or using targeted strategies like Roth conversions can work even better.

Research by retirement expert Wade Pfau shows that incorporating tax-efficient withdrawal strategies, such as blending account types and strategically timing Roth conversions, can extend a portfolio's longevity by more than five years compared to a conventional withdrawal order alone [1]. In other words, the right strategy can provide more financial security throughout retirement without requiring you to save more or take additional investment risk.

THE STRATEGIC USE OF ROTH CONVERSIONS

A Roth conversion involves moving money from a traditional IRA or 401(k) into a Roth IRA. When you do so, you pay taxes on the converted amount in the year of the conversion, but future growth and withdrawals become tax-free. This can be a powerful strategy for retirees who are in a temporarily low tax bracket or those looking to reduce the size of their future RMDs.

However, Roth conversions come with tradeoffs. If you convert too much in a single year, you may push yourself into a higher tax bracket, trigger Medicare surcharges (IRMAA), or even affect Social Security taxation. It is important to understand how the tax bill is calculated before proceeding.

How Roth Conversion Taxes Are Calculated:
- The amount converted is added to your taxable income for the year
- It is taxed at your ordinary income tax rate
- It may cause your marginal tax bracket to increase
- It may also affect Medicare premiums or eligibility for tax credits

For example, a retiree with $60,000 in other taxable income who converts $40,000 from a traditional IRA could find themselves bumped into a higher tax bracket, depending on their filing status. This extra income could also increase Medicare Part B and Part D premiums by pushing them over the IRMAA threshold.

Since Roth conversions are now permanent and cannot be undone (due to a 2018 tax law change), it is crucial to model out the tax consequences before moving forward.

A more measured approach often involves filling up a lower tax bracket over a series of years. For instance, if your income is low enough to keep you in the 12 percent bracket, you might convert just enough to reach the top of that bracket, then stop for the year. This spreads the tax cost out and helps prevent unintended jumps in taxes and premiums.

Tax and legal considerations vary by individual. Consult a qualified tax advisor or attorney before making decisions.

UNDERSTANDING ROTH CONVERSIONS VS. BACKDOOR ROTH IRAS

It is important to distinguish between a Roth conversion and a backdoor Roth contribution. While both result in funds ending up in a Roth IRA, they serve different purposes and follow different tax paths.

- A **Roth conversion** involves moving pre-tax money from a traditional IRA or 401(k) into a Roth IRA. This is a taxable event. The converted amount is added to your income for the year and taxed at your ordinary income tax rate.
- A **backdoor Roth contribution** is a workaround for high-income earners who are ineligible to contribute directly to a Roth IRA. It involves making a non-deductible contribution to a traditional IRA, then converting that amount to a Roth IRA. While the contribution itself is not taxed, any earnings before conversion or other pre-tax IRA balances can make part of the conversion taxable under the IRS pro-rata rule [4].

Each approach has its own risks. With Roth conversions, converting too much in one year can push your income into a higher tax bracket and increase Medicare premiums. With backdoor Roths, timing errors or misunderstanding the pro-rata rule can lead to unexpected tax consequences [2].

Tax and legal considerations vary by individual. Consult a qualified tax advisor or attorney before making decisions.

QUALIFIED CHARITABLE DISTRIBUTIONS (QCDS): GIVE STRATEGICALLY, PAY LESS IN TAXES

Another powerful strategy for tax efficiency is the Qualified Charitable Distribution. If you are age 70½ or older, you can give up to $100,000 per year directly from your IRA to a qualified charity. This counts toward your RMD once you reach age 73, but does not count as taxable income on your return.

Why this matters: Reducing your adjusted gross income (AGI) can help avoid tax bracket creep, lower Medicare premiums, and reduce taxes on Social Security benefits. Even if you no longer itemize deductions under current tax law, a QCD gives you a direct income reduction, making it one of the few ways to give and save taxes at the same time.

For retirees who do not need their full RMD for spending, QCDs can be a great way to make a charitable impact and reduce their tax bill at the same time.

Key Takeaways: Tax-Efficient Withdrawal Strategies
- Withdrawing from taxable accounts first, then tax-deferred, and finally Roth accounts can reduce your long-term tax burden
- Roth conversions can be valuable, but doing them carelessly can lead to higher taxes and Medicare costs
- Backdoor Roths are a different strategy with their own tax implications. Timing and account structure matter
- QCDs allow charitably inclined retirees to reduce taxable income without needing to itemize deductions

- Structured withdrawal strategies have been shown to increase the longevity of retirement portfolios by several years

Tax and legal considerations vary by individual. Consult a qualified tax advisor or attorney before making decisions.

DIVERSIFIED INCOME STREAMS: WAYS TO LAYER RETIREMENT PAYCHECKS

Before we dive into building your retirement paycheck in Chapter 8, it is important to step back and understand the different types of income that can make up a retirement plan. Most retirees do not rely on just one income source. Instead, retirement income is often layered across multiple sources, some guaranteed, and some variable, to create stability, flexibility, and tax efficiency over time.

Understanding these sources at a high level can help you make better decisions and recognize where your income gaps might be. It also helps explain why two people with similar savings can have very different retirement outcomes depending on how their income is structured.

Let's take a closer look at some common income sources to evaluate when building a plan.

SOCIAL SECURITY: A FOUNDATION WITH BUILT-IN INFLATION PROTECTION

Social Security is often the cornerstone of a retirement income plan. For many people, it is the only guaranteed income stream with built-in inflation adjustments. This makes it especially valuable over a 20- or 30-year retirement.

Unlike most pensions or annuities, Social Security includes annual cost-of-living adjustments (COLAs), which help offset the rising cost of goods and services. This inflation protection makes Social Security a critical source of secure, long-term income that grows over time.

Tax treatment: Depending on your total income, up to 85 percent of your Social Security benefit may be subject to income tax. The calculation is based on your "combined income," which includes your adjusted gross income, nontaxable interest, and half of your Social Security benefit [3].

PENSIONS: RELIABLE BUT OFTEN FIXED

Pensions are becoming less common in the private sector, but many public employees and some long-time corporate workers still receive them. Pensions often provide regular monthly payments for life, usually based on your salary and years of service.

Unlike Social Security, most pensions do not increase with inflation. That means a $2,000 per month pension might feel secure early in retirement but could lose purchasing power over time as prices rise.

Tax treatment: Pension income is typically taxed as ordinary income.

ANNUITIES: FILLING THE GAPS

Annuities can provide guaranteed income for life or for a set number of years. They are issued by insurance companies, and payments are subject to the claims-paying ability of the insurer.

Some retirees use annuities to supplement other income sources or to cover a specific need. One approach is using an annuity to generate income in the early years of retirement while delaying Social Security to maximize future benefits. This can create predictable cash flow while giving their Social Security benefit time to grow.

Tax treatment: Annuity payments may be partially taxable if funded with after-tax dollars. The taxable portion represents earnings. If funded with pre-tax dollars (like from a traditional IRA), then 100 percent of the payments are taxed as ordinary income.

The guarantee of the annuity is backed by the claims paying ability of the issuing insurance company.

IRA WITHDRAWALS: TAXABLE BUT FLEXIBLE

Withdrawals from traditional IRAs and 401(k)s are often a primary income source in retirement. These accounts offer flexibility, but the timing and amount of withdrawals must be managed carefully to avoid unnecessary taxes or running out of funds too early.

Beginning at age 73, required minimum distributions (RMDs) must be taken from traditional retirement accounts. Withdrawals taken before this point are sometimes coordinated to fill lower tax brackets, particularly when considering Roth conversions or the timing of Social Security income.

Tax treatment: Withdrawals from traditional IRAs and 401(k)s are fully taxable as ordinary income.

DIVIDENDS AND INTEREST: VARIABLE BUT POTENTIALLY USEFUL

Some retirees rely on investment income from stocks and bonds to support their lifestyle. This includes qualified dividends, which are often taxed at lower rates, and bond interest, which is taxed as ordinary income.

While these income sources can supplement a retirement plan, they are less predictable than guaranteed income. Dividends can be reduced or suspended, and interest rates fluctuate with the economy.

Tax treatment:

- Qualified dividends: Taxed at long-term capital gains rates (0%, 15%, or 20% depending on income) [4].

- Interest income: Taxed as ordinary income.

RENTAL INCOME: A SUPPLEMENTAL OPTION

Real estate can provide monthly income and long-term appreciation. However, being a landlord comes with responsibilities and potential volatility. For some retirees, rental properties provide steady cash flow. For others, the management burden outweighs the benefit.

Rental income is one of several tools that might be used to support retirement, but it is not a focus of this book.

Tax treatment: Rental income is taxable, but you can deduct expenses such as mortgage interest, property taxes, maintenance, and depreciation.

RETIREMENT INCOME COMPARISON

The chart below compares key attributes of common retirement income sources to help illustrate their differences in guarantees, taxation, inflation protection, and risk.

Income Source	Guaranteed?	Taxable?	Inflation Protection	Liquidity	Common Risks
Social Security	Yes	Up to 85%	Yes (COLA)	No	Claiming too early
Pension	Yes	Yes	Rarely	No	Funding shortfall
Annuity	Yes	Yes	Not usually	No	Insurer risk
IRA Withdrawals	No	Yes	No	Yes	Market volatility
Dividends	No	Yes	No	Yes	Dividend cuts
Rental Income	No	Yes	Variable	Medium	Vacancy or repairs

Comparing Two Income Scenarios

To illustrate how income sources can vary, consider these two examples:

Jane has:

- Social Security: $2,200/month
- A pension from her years in public service: $1,500/month
- A small annuity providing $500/month

Jane has $4,200/month in reliable, predictable income. She feels confident covering her essential expenses and does not worry much about market volatility.

Tom, on the other hand, relies on:

- Social Security: $2,000/month
- Withdrawals from his traditional IRA
- Dividends from a taxable investment account

Tom's monthly income is less predictable. He adjusts his IRA withdrawals each year based on market performance and is more sensitive to investment losses or inflation shocks. While he has flexibility, this approach requires greater discipline during market downturns.

Both Jane and Tom have reasonable plans, but they will experience retirement differently. Jane's steady income gives her confidence. Tom values flexibility but needs a tighter plan.

These figures are hypothetical and for illustrative purposes only. Actual results will vary and are not guaranteed

KEY TAKEAWAYS: RETIREMENT INCOME SOURCES

- Most retirees benefit from combining multiple income sources rather than relying on one
- Social Security is one of the few income sources with built-in inflation protection
- Pensions and annuities provide stability but may not keep up with inflation
- IRA withdrawals and dividends offer flexibility but require active management
- A thoughtful income blend supports both spending confidence and long-term financial sustainability

ALTERNATIVE INVESTMENTS: A HIGH-LEVEL OVERVIEW

As investors seek to diversify beyond traditional stocks and bonds, alternative investments have gained attention. These assets, ranging from private equity to commodities to cryptocurrency, offer potential benefits but come with unique risks. Understanding their characteristics is crucial before incorporating them into an investment plan.

This section is not intended to be an extensive deep dive into each type of alternative investment. Due to the complexity and technical details involved, such a level of analysis would go beyond the scope of this book. Instead, this is a high-level overview designed to help readers understand the broad categories, common risks, and general considerations that come into play when evaluating alternative investments.

UNDERSTANDING ALTERNATIVE INVESTMENTS

Alternative investments encompass a broad category of assets outside conventional investments. Common types include:

- **Private Equity**: Investments in private companies, often through venture capital or buyouts
- **Hedge Funds**: Pooled funds employing diverse strategies to earn active returns
- **Real Estate**: Direct property ownership or indirect investments like REITs
- **Commodities**: Physical goods such as gold, oil, or agricultural products
- **Cryptocurrencies**: Digital or virtual currencies using cryptography for security
- **Structured Notes**: Debt securities with returns linked to the performance of an underlying asset

These investments often promise higher returns or diversification benefits. However, they typically involve higher fees, less liquidity, and greater complexity than traditional investments [5].

RISKS AND CONSIDERATIONS

Illiquidity: Many alternative investments cannot be easily sold or converted to cash. For example, non-traded REITs may restrict redemptions, leaving investors unable to access funds when needed. Some investors learned this the hard way during the 2008 financial crisis when numerous non-traded REITs suspended dividend payments and became extremely difficult to sell. Years later, many investors were still unable to access their money.

This scenario can become more problematic when non-traded REITs are held in retirement accounts. Investors who reach Required Minimum

Distribution (RMD) age must take distributions, even if the asset itself cannot be sold for cash. While it is possible to transfer shares out of the IRA to satisfy the distribution requirement, this does not generate cash to pay the associated taxes. Without advance planning, this can put retirees in a difficult financial position.

High Fees: Alternatives often carry substantial fees. Hedge funds, for example, may charge a 2 percent management fee plus 20 percent of profits, which can significantly erode returns over time.

Complexity: Understanding the structure and risks of alternative investments requires significant due diligence. Misunderstanding these investments can lead to unexpected losses [5].

Regulatory Oversight: Some alternatives lack the regulatory scrutiny of traditional investments, potentially increasing risk.

ACADEMIC AND REGULATORY PERSPECTIVES

Research indicates that while alternative investments can offer diversification benefits, they may underperform traditional portfolios when accounting for fees and liquidity constraints. Richard Ennis found that large endowments heavily invested in alternatives did not outperform a simple 60/40 stock-bond portfolio, partly due to high costs and complexity [6].

Regulatory bodies like FINRA have issued guidance emphasizing the need for thorough due diligence when recommending alternative investments. Firms are advised to ensure that clients understand the risks and that such investments align with their financial goals and risk tolerance [7]. These factors help explain why alternative investments may not be appropriate for all investors or for every investment strategy.

COMPARATIVE OVERVIEW

Below is a summary of key characteristics of various alternative investments:

Investment Type	Liquidity	Typical Fees	Complexity	Regulatory Oversight	Suitable For
Private Equity	Low	High	High	Limited	Long-term investors
Hedge Funds	Low	High	High	Moderate	Accredited investors
Real Estate	Medium	Medium	Medium	Varies	Income-focused investors
Commodities	High	Low	Medium	High	Diversification seekers
Cryptocurrencies	High	Low	High	Limited	Speculative investors
Structured Notes	Low	Medium	High	High	Yield-focused investors

Note: This table is a general guide. Individual investment characteristics may vary.

*Cetera does not offer any direct investments, endorsement, or advice as it relates to Bitcoin or any crypto currency. This Is for Information purposes only.

FINAL THOUGHTS

Alternative investments can play a role in a diversified portfolio, offering potential benefits like non-correlation with traditional markets. However, their complexities, fees, and liquidity constraints require careful evaluation. Understanding these tradeoffs is essential when determining whether alternative investments fit within a broader investment strategy.

References

1. Wade Pfau, "Tax-Efficient Withdrawal Strategies," Bogleheads® Chapter Series. https://boglecenter.net/bogleheads-chapter-series-wade-pfau-on-retirement-income-style-analysis-tax-efficiency

2. Forbes. "What Is A Backdoor Roth IRA?" https://www.forbes.com/advisor/retirement/backdoor-roth-ira/

3. Social Security Administration. Understanding the Benefits (Publication No. EN-05-10024). U.S. Social Security Administration, January 2025, pp. 11. https://www.ssa.gov/pubs/EN-05-10024.pdf

4. Vanguard. How Are Dividends Taxed? Investor Resources & Education — Taxes. https://investor.vanguard.com/investor-resources-education/taxes/dividends

5. Investopedia. The Pros and Cons of Alternative Investments. Investopedia, updated September 25, 2024. https://www.investopedia.com/articles/financial-advisors/092515/alternative-investments-look-pros-cons.asp

6. Ennis, Richard M. The Endowment Syndrome: Why Elite Funds Are Falling Behind. December 6, 2024. https://richardmennis.com/blog/the-endowment-syndrome-why-elite-funds-are-falling-behind

7. ☐ FINRA. "Regulatory Notice 22-11: Heightened Supervision of Alternative Investments." https://www.finra.org/rules-guidance/notices/22-11

CHAPTER 8
BUILDING A RETIREMENT INCOME PLAN

Retirement marks the beginning of a new financial phase, not the end of financial planning. While accumulating assets is a significant achievement, the challenge lies in transforming those assets into a sustainable income stream that designed to navigate market fluctuations, inflation, and the uncertainties of longevity. Building a retirement income plan is rarely a one-time decision. It's an ongoing process that requires regular assessment and adjustment to align with your needs, goals, account types, tax considerations, and investment preferences.

In this chapter, we'll walk through the big picture of retirement income planning. You'll learn about widely used strategies, how your preferences shape which approach may fit best, and where the planning gets more complicated. This is not a blueprint for building your own retirement income plan. Instead, it's a framework to help you understand the moving pieces and the kind of thinking that goes into designing an income plan intended to support you for the long run.

WHY INCOME PLANNING IS SO COMPLEX

A good retirement income strategy is rarely something you set and forget. Your spending needs may change. Markets will go up and down. Health expenses can appear unexpectedly. Tax laws shift. Without a plan that adapts, even well-funded retirees can face financial stress. Several key risks make this type of planning especially challenging.

1. Sequence of Returns Risk

When you retire, the timing of your investment returns becomes just as important as the returns themselves. If the market performs poorly early in retirement while you're taking withdrawals, your savings can shrink faster than expected. Even if strong returns come later, they may not be enough to recover what was lost. This is why early-retirement market downturns can have a much bigger impact on your long-term income plan than similar downturns during your working years.

Example: Two retirees each start with $100,000 and withdraw 5% per year, adjusted for inflation. One retires in 1969 and experiences negative returns in four of the first ten years, along with high inflation. The other retires in 1979 and faces negative returns in only two of the first ten years. Despite the first retiree having a higher average return, their portfolio is depleted after just 15 years, while the second retiree's portfolio continues to grow.[1]

Visual: *Sequence of Returns Risk Chart*

Age	Mr. Smith Investment: $100,000 Stocks 60% | Bonds 40% Retired 1/1/1969 – Annual withdrawals: $5,000			Ms. Jones Investment: $100,000 Stocks 60% | Bonds 40% Retired 1/1/1979 – Annual withdrawals: $5,000		
	Year	ROR	Year-end value	Year	ROR	Year-end value
65	1969	-2.6%	$92,168	1979	14.7%	$109,172
66	1970	5.3%	$91,449	1980	23.9%	$128,899
67	1971	10.5%	$95,219	1981	3.4%	$126,282
68	1972	12.9%	$101,447	1982	16.6%	$139,848
69	1973	-6.6%	$88,410	1983	16.6%	$155,426
70	1974	-12.6%	$70,219	1984	7.3%	$158,880
71	1975	25.1%	$80,085	1985	22.0%	$185,630
72	1976	16.5%	$85,107	1986	13.9%	$203,223
73	1977	-2.4%	$74,324	1987	5.7%	$206,232
74	1978	6.3%	$69,660	1988	12.2%	$222,537
75	1979	14.7%	$69,487	1989	22.1%	$262,402
76	1980	23.9%	$74,222	1990	1.2%	$255,753
77	1981	3.4%	$63,670	1991	20.8%	$298,808
78	1982	16.6%	$60,391	1992	6.1%	$306,574
79	1983	16.6%	$56,145	1993	7.3%	$318,026
80	1984	7.3%	$45,480	1994	2.0%	$313,351
81	1985	22.0%	$40,198	1995	24.6%	$378,884
82	1986	13.9%	$30,286	1996	16.3%	$429,072
83	1987	5.7%	$15,941	1997	21.1%	$507,502
84	1988	12.2%	$1,176	1998	19.1%	$592,094
85	1989	22.1%	Exhausted	1999	14.3%	$664,249
86	1990	1.2%	Exhausted	2000	-0.8%	$645,969
87	1991	20.8%	Exhausted	2001	-3.8%	$608,120
88	1992	6.1%	Exhausted	2002	-9.3%	$538,413
89	1993	7.3%	Exhausted	2003	18.9%	$626,319
90	1994	2.0%	Exhausted	2004	8.2%	$663,790
91	1995	24.6%	Exhausted	2005	3.8%	$674,761
92	1996	16.3%	Exhausted	2006	11.2%	$735,149
93	1997	21.1%	Exhausted	2007	6.1%	$764,278
94	1998	19.1%	Exhausted	2008	-20.5%	$591,402
	Average ROR 10.5%			**Average ROR 9.6%**		

When You Retire Makes a Difference
■ Mr. Smith
■ Ms. Jones

Source: Financial Perspectives. "Sequence of Returns Risk and Retirement." March 18, 2015. Available at: https://www.financialperspectives.biz/perspectives-retirement-blog/gc1i1jbbe90kg2rxggrpk7hugeva73

These figures are hypothetical and for illustrative purposes only. Actual results will vary and are not guaranteed.

This example highlights how the timing of returns during withdrawal years can significantly influence the outcome of a retirement plan. Early losses reduce the base from which future gains can grow, and because you're withdrawing funds, there's less left to recover.

2. Inflation Risk

Over time, inflation erodes the purchasing power of your money. While inflation may seem modest from year to year, its compounding effect over 20 to 30 years can be significant.

Example: In 1980, the average cost of a new car was about $7,200. By 2020, it was over $37,000 — more than five times as much [2].

Even modest inflation of 2.5 percent annually can double your living expenses over a 30-year retirement. If income doesn't keep pace with rising costs, purchasing power can gradually decline over time.

3. Longevity Risk

People are living longer than ever. That is good news, but it also increases the chances that your money needs to last 30 or even 40 years. Today's 65-year-olds often face a retirement horizon of 20-25 years (or more), thanks to improvements in longevity as shown by official life tables, which implies their savings may need to last into their 80s or beyond [3]. That means your plan needs to be built to last, with room for adjustment and flexibility.

WHAT RETIREES MIGHT MISS

Financial advisors often work with planning tools and frameworks that may not be well known to DIY retirees such as:

- **Cash flow modeling** to map income needs and investment drawdowns over time
- **Tax-efficient withdrawal planning** based on account type and asset location
- **Software platforms**, including:

- *eMoney* and *MoneyGuidePro*, which help visualize goals, income layers, and tax impacts
- *Monte Carlo simulations*, which test thousands of market scenarios to estimate your plan's chance of success
- *RISA (Retirement Income Style Awareness)*, which helps align your income plan with your personal preferences

While these tools can be helpful, the value lies less in the software itself and more in the underlying concepts they illustrate. Used thoughtfully, these tools do more than provide numbers. They can help reduce uncertainty by illustrating tradeoffs and possibilities. Retirement planning is not just about solving a math problem, it is about helping you feel secure through market cycles, tax changes, and life transitions.

IT IS MORE EMOTIONAL THAN IT SEEMS

Fear of running out of money is one of the most common concerns retirees face. And that fear is not irrational. When income planning lacks clarity, people often react emotionally, cutting spending unnecessarily or making poor investment decisions during market declines. A well-structured plan offers more than just projections. It can support peace of mind during uncertain periods.

UNDERSTANDING YOUR RETIREMENT INCOME STYLE

WHAT IS RISA?

The Retirement Income Style Awareness (RISA) is a tool developed by retirement researchers Wade Pfau and Alex Murguia to help individuals identify their preferences for generating income in retirement. Unlike traditional risk tolerance questionnaires, RISA focuses on how you prefer to source your retirement income, considering factors such as flexibility, commitment, and your comfort with market-based versus guaranteed income [4].

RISA is not an investment product and does not recommend specific investments. It is a diagnostic tool designed to help you better understand your mindset around retirement income. That understanding can guide the structure of your income plan, helping align your retirement strategy with how you actually think and feel about generating income.

THE FOUR RETIREMENT INCOME STYLES

RISA identifies four primary retirement income styles. Each represents a different way people prefer to manage the tradeoffs between flexibility, predictability, and market risk in retirement. These styles can help guide which income approach may feel most natural to you.

RISA Style	Description	Associated Income Approach
Total Return	Prefers flexibility and is comfortable relying on market growth for income.	Total Return
Income Protection	Seeks safety and is inclined toward guaranteed income sources like annuities.	Flooring
Risk Wrap	Desires market participation but with protective features to guard against significant downside risk.	Risk Wrap
Time Segmentation	Likes dividing retirement into stages, using short-term safe assets and long-term growth investments to align income with different time horizons.	Bucket

These are not rigid boxes. Many people share elements of more than one style, and some households include spouses with different preferences. But knowing where you generally fall can help you choose a retirement income structure that makes sense for you.

REFLECTION QUESTIONS

To begin identifying your style, consider how you would answer the following questions:

- **Total Return**: Do you prefer keeping control of your investments and adjusting your income over time based on market performance?
- **Income Protection**: Would you feel more confident in retirement if your essential expenses were covered by guaranteed sources of income?
- **Risk Wrap**: Are you interested in the potential growth of the stock market but want some built-in protection against big losses?
- **Time Segmentation**: Does it make sense to you to separate your savings into short-, medium-, and long-term buckets based on when you'll need the money?

You don't need to take a formal assessment to begin understanding your preferences, but these questions can help you think more clearly about the approach that may suit you best.

If you'd like a more personalized way to explore your style, you can take a short questionnaire created by the researchers who developed the RISA. It's available free of charge at:
https://retirementresearcher.com/landing/risa/

YOUR PREFERENCES CAN CHANGE

Like many things in life, your income preferences can shift over time. Market volatility, health changes, loss of a spouse, or even evolving goals can cause someone to lean more conservative or flexible than they originally thought. That's why good income planning is rarely a one-and-done. It's a process that should adapt alongside you.

FROM PREFERENCES TO PLANNING

Now that you've seen how retirement income styles reflect personal preferences, it's time to connect those preferences to real planning strategies. Each income approach we'll explore aligns with one of the four RISA styles. However, it's rarely a perfect one-to-one match.

Many retirees find they relate to a combination of approaches. For example, someone might feel confident using investments to generate income, but also want a portion of their basic expenses covered by guaranteed sources. That's perfectly normal. Many people prefer a blend of income approaches that reflects their comfort level, income needs, and financial goals. As you read through the following sections, consider which elements might resonate with you and how a blended strategy could reflect the way you think about risk, income stability, and flexibility.

Your preferences aren't fixed either. They can change over time as life unfolds, whether through market volatility, a health event, or simply gaining more clarity about what retirement feels like in practice. What tends to matter most is building an income plan that reflects how you think about money and how much certainty or flexibility you want in retirement.

The next few sections will walk through four primary income approaches as outlined by RISA: Total Return, Income Protection, Risk Wrap, and Bucket. These aren't product recommendations or cookie-cutter plans. They're frameworks. By understanding how each works, you'll be better equipped to think through what makes sense for your situation or mix elements of each to create a more personal fit.

TOTAL RETURN APPROACH

The Total Return approach is a retirement income strategy that closely resembles how many individuals save during their working years. It involves maintaining a diversified investment portfolio, typically made up of stocks, bonds, and other assets, and systematically withdrawing funds to meet income needs. This method often uses tax-advantaged accounts like 401(k)s, IRAs, or Roth IRAs, where selling investments does not immediately trigger taxes.

Income in a Total Return strategy is usually generated by periodically rebalancing the portfolio and selling assets to raise cash for withdrawals. Common withdrawal methods include the 4 percent rule, where retirees begin by withdrawing 4 percent of the portfolio's value in the first year of retirement and then increase that amount annually to keep up with inflation. Others may prefer a fixed dollar withdrawal method, where a set amount is taken each month or year regardless of market performance. Dynamic withdrawal strategies offer another option by adjusting the income taken based on how the portfolio performs. In strong market years, a retiree may be able to take more, while in weak years, they might reduce withdrawals to preserve long-term viability. These approaches aim to provide sustainable income while maintaining flexibility.

This approach often fits retirees who prefer simplicity, value flexibility, and are comfortable with some market risk. It also appeals to those who have saved primarily in one large account such as a 401(k) or IRA and are used to managing investments in that way. According to research by Murguía and Pfau, approximately 33 percent of individuals preparing for retirement are most aligned with the Total Return approach [5].

Common characteristics of the Total Return strategy include flexibility, growth potential, tax deferral, and a simplified structure. Retirees have the freedom to adjust withdrawals as needed and can benefit from long-term growth in a well-diversified portfolio. Utilizing tax-advantaged accounts can help reduce or delay taxes, and managing one large account is often easier than juggling multiple sources of income. However, this method also comes with challenges.

Sequence of returns risk is a primary concern. Experiencing poor market performance early in retirement can significantly reduce the long-term viability of the portfolio. Because there are no guaranteed income sources built into the strategy, market downturns can create uncertainty. Retirees may feel pressure to change course during volatility, which is why behavioral discipline becomes essential. This strategy tends to function best when withdrawals are adjusted thoughtfully rather than in reaction to short-term market movements.

Managing a Total Return strategy typically requires ongoing attention and decision-making. This may include monitoring portfolio performance, maintaining a consistent withdrawal strategy, and adjusting based on market conditions or changing personal needs. It also involves tax-aware planning, knowing how and when to draw from different types of accounts to minimize taxes over time. Regular rebalancing is important to keep the portfolio aligned with your intended level of risk. For many, the challenge is not just investment management but staying disciplined during market downturns. A well-structured plan, reviewed regularly, may help ensure income needs are met without overreacting to short-term volatility.

For example, a retiree with a $1 million investment portfolio might use the 4 percent rule to withdraw $40,000 in the first year, adjusting that amount for inflation in subsequent years. If the market performs well, the portfolio may grow even while supporting income needs. If the market drops early in retirement, the retiree may choose to temporarily reduce withdrawals or reevaluate spending to preserve the portfolio's longevity. This highlights the importance of having a strategy that can adapt to changing conditions while remaining rooted in long-term discipline.

INCOME PROTECTION APPROACH

The Income Protection approach, often referred to as the "flooring" or "safety-first" strategy, focuses on structuring income so that a retiree's essential expenses are covered by reliable, predictable income sources. This method distinguishes between needs such as housing, food, and utilities and wants, which include discretionary expenses like vacations, new vehicles, or gifts for grandchildren.

Implementing this strategy starts with estimating the monthly income required to meet basic needs and then identifying guaranteed income sources to cover that amount. Common sources include Social Security, pensions, and annuities. Social Security typically adjusts for inflation, while pensions and annuities may not, so it's important to factor in potential cost-of-living increases when planning.

This approach appeals to individuals who prefer a conservative strategy, valuing the assurance that their essential expenses will be met regardless of market fluctuations. According to research by Murguía and Pfau, approximately 35 percent of individuals preparing for retirement resonate with the Income Protection approach [5].

Common characteristics of the Income Protection strategy include:

- **Psychological comfort**: Having greater confidence that basic needs are largely covered may reduce anxiety about market volatility
- **Reduced sequence of returns risk**: By securing essential income, retirees are less vulnerable to the timing of market downturns
- **Simplified budgeting**: Having your basic needs covered by a reliable income floor allows more flexibility in planning for wants

However, there are challenges to consider:

- **Defining needs vs. wants**: Determining what constitutes a "need" can be subjective. For some, certain expenses like a comprehensive cable package may feel essential.
- **Potentially lower returns**: Allocating funds to guaranteed income products might result in lower overall investment returns.
- **Reduced liquidity and flexibility**: Products like annuities can limit access to funds, making it harder to respond to unexpected expenses.

Common income sources used in this strategy include:

- **Social Security**: Timing decisions can impact the amount received.

- **Annuities**: Lifetime or fixed-term annuities can provide steady income.
- **Pensions**: For those with defined benefit plans, choosing the right payout option is an important decision.

It's important to note that while this strategy is designed to provide a stable foundation, it can be combined with other approaches to address discretionary spending needs. We'll explore blending strategies later in this chapter.

RISK WRAP APPROACH

The Risk Wrap approach integrates investment growth potential with income guarantees. It appeals to retirees who want both participation in market growth and a sense of protection against the risk of running out of money. This strategy typically uses variable annuities or equity-indexed annuities, both of which can include features such as Guaranteed Lifetime Withdrawal Benefits (GLWBs). These products allow retirees to invest in the market or an index-linked option while securing a predictable income stream, regardless of market performance [6]. These guarantees are subject to the claims paying ability of the insurance company that issues the product.

Unlike the Income Protection strategy, which focuses on meeting essential needs through guaranteed sources like Social Security or fixed annuities, the Risk Wrap approach adds a growth component. By incorporating annuities that allow for market or index participation, retirees can balance the comfort of guaranteed income with the potential for higher long-term returns.

RISA research shows that about 15 percent of retirement investors identify with the Risk Wrap approach [5]. These individuals tend to favor commitment-based income strategies while still being open to investment-based solutions.

In practice, Risk Wrap planning might involve using a portion of total retirement assets, often around 30 percent, to purchase an annuity with guaranteed income features. This allows retirees to protect part of their income stream while keeping other assets liquid and flexible.

Common characteristics of the Risk Wrap Approach

- **Market participation with downside protection**: Retirees can grow their assets while protecting against sequence-of-returns risk through guaranteed income.
- **Predictable income stream**: GLWB riders ensure a base level of income that cannot be outlived.
- **Maintains some liquidity**: Unlike full annuitization, risk wrap strategies typically allow continued access to account value.

Risks and Considerations

- **Product complexity**: Annuities with income guarantees often involve detailed rules, riders, and contractual limitations.
- **Fees and expenses**: These annuities typically carry higher costs than traditional investments.
- **Insurance company risk**: The guarantees rely on the claims-paying ability of the insurer.
- **Limited growth potential**: Although there is upside participation, caps or participation rates may limit returns in strong markets.

Implementation Considerations

- **Income need assessment**: Determine what portion of monthly expenses you may want to cover with guarantees through an annuity income

- **Product selection**: Choose between variable and indexed annuities based on personal preference and risk tolerance

- **Asset allocation**: Decide how much of your overall retirement portfolio you choose to allocate to these types of products

This strategy tends to appeal to individuals who value stability but do not want to give up entirely on investment growth. It can provide emotional comfort while still leaving room for flexibility. As always, any retirement income plan ideally reflects your specific goals, needs, and comfort with risk.

TIME SEGMENTATION (BUCKET STRATEGY)

The Time Segmentation strategy, also known as the bucket strategy, organizes retirement assets by the time horizon in which they'll be used. Each "bucket" is matched to a spending need within a different time frame, allowing retirees to align their investment risk with how soon the funds will be needed. This approach is intended to help reduce emotional stress about short-term market volatility by ensuring that the money needed soon is not exposed to market downturns.

Common characteristics of this strategy uses three buckets:

- **Bucket 1: Immediate Needs (0–3 years)**
  This bucket contains very conservative investments like cash, short-term bonds, and money market funds. Its purpose is to fund near-term income needs with little exposure to market fluctuations. For example, if a retiree expects to withdraw $3,000 per month, they might allocate about $108,000 here to cover three years of income needs.

- **Bucket 2: Intermediate Needs (4–9 years)**
  This bucket holds a mix of equity and fixed income investments, often structured like a traditional 60/40 portfolio. The idea is to grow the funds modestly while still managing volatility. If the retiree needs another $3,000 per month over this six-year period, they might place roughly $200,000 here.

- **Bucket 3: Long-Term Needs (10+ years)**
  The third bucket is invested for growth, typically in stocks or equity-heavy funds. Because these funds won't be touched for a decade or more, they have time to recover from market downturns. The long-term bucket is periodically tapped to refill the other two as money is spent.

One commonly cited benefit of this strategy is the psychological comfort it provides. Having the next several years of spending are already set aside in conservative investments can help retirees stay calm during market downturns. The structured rebalancing between buckets also reinforces disciplined investing behavior.

Sequence of returns risk may be reduced because the retiree is less likely to withdraw from their long-term, equity-heavy investments during those critical early years.

Challenges of the Time Segmentation Approach

One challenge is complexity. While the concept sounds straightforward, deciding how much to place in each bucket and when to refill them requires thoughtful planning. Some retirees also try to time the markets when deciding when to refill buckets, which can add unnecessary stress and risk. A simplified rule, such as reviewing buckets annually and refilling as needed, is often the practical approach.

This strategy does not usually rely on guaranteed income sources like annuities. Outside of Social Security, the income is drawn entirely from investment assets. That makes diversification, discipline, and rebalancing especially important.

The time segmentation approach is sometimes confused with the total return approach. Both rely on investment assets rather than guarantees, but time segmentation adds structure by aligning different parts of the portfolio with different time horizons.

Who Might Prefer This Approach?

This strategy tends to appeal to individuals who value organization and want to match their income planning with time-based goals. It provides a visual and mental framework for managing risk and income needs. According to the RISA study, approximately 17% of individuals identify most closely with the Time Segmentation income style [5].

BLENDING RETIREMENT INCOME APPROACHES

We've covered the four core strategies for structuring retirement withdrawals: Total Return, Income Protection (Flooring), Risk Wrap, and Time Segmentation (Bucket Strategy). While each can stand on its own, many retirees don't fit perfectly into just one. Blending multiple strategies is both common and often reflects how people actually think about retirement income.

135

As you've reviewed each option, you may have found yourself drawn to features from more than one strategy. That's completely normal. In many cases, blending approaches can feel more realistic than sticking to just one model. Everyone's financial life is unique, and that means their retirement income plan should reflect their comfort level, needs, and preferences.

There's no single "right" combination. For example, one common pairing is using a flooring strategy to establish secure income through Social Security and possibly an annuity, then using a Total Return approach for the rest of the portfolio. This structure can help support confidence around essential expenses while allowing for growth and flexibility elsewhere.

For example, someone might use Social Security and a fixed annuity to establish a base layer of secure income (a Flooring approach), while investing the rest of their portfolio using a Total Return strategy to cover discretionary expenses and pursue growth. Another person might use Time Segmentation to manage investment risk based on when funds are needed, while allocating a portion of their assets to a variable or indexed annuity with guaranteed income features, a nod to the Risk Wrap approach.

The key here is simplicity. While blending can be effective, trying to combine too many elements can overcomplicate the plan. Choose one primary approach that resonates with you, then consider adding a secondary strategy to complement it. Avoid the temptation to blend every possible technique. A plan that's too complex can be harder to manage and may increase the risk of costly missteps.

For couples, blending strategies can also mean finding common ground between different comfort levels. If one spouse favors a more conservative, protected income strategy and the other prefers a market-based approach, it may make sense to assign different accounts to different roles. For example, one partner's IRA could follow a Total Return strategy while the other's is allocated using Time Segmentation. Together, they can form a unified plan that reflects both personalities.

In practice, blending retirement income strategies can offer flexibility and personalization. It allows for a plan that fits your needs, not just at the start of retirement, but over time as your goals and circumstances evolve.

Reflection Questions:

- Which strategy felt most natural to you as you read the earlier sections?
- Are there aspects of multiple strategies you'd like to incorporate?
- How important is having guaranteed income for your essential spending?
- How much control do you want over your investments and withdrawals?
- Could a simple blend of strategies give you more peace of mind?

All investing involves risk, including the possible loss of principal. There is no assurance that any investment strategy will be successful.

CREATING YOUR RETIREMENT PAYCHECK

What is a retirement paycheck? It's the stream of income that supports your lifestyle after you stop working. During your career, income typically arrives on a regular schedule. In retirement, the responsibility shifts to you: your savings and income sources are gradually converted into a cash flow intended to support your lifestyle. This involves understanding where that income will come from and how it will be generated.

Many people retire with a pool of money in accounts like IRAs, 401(k)s, or taxable accounts. The challenge becomes how to turn that lump sum into an income stream that will be expected to cover your needs and wants for potentially decades. The process starts with clarity around your spending. While few people enjoy budgeting, having at least a basic understanding of monthly expenses provides a useful foundation so you can estimate how much income may need to be withdrawn.

That includes accounting for different billing cycles (monthly, quarterly, annually) and being realistic about inflation. Costs won't stay static over time. A good retirement plan should reflect how your expenses will change as you age, and how inflation may erode purchasing power. Financial planning software like eMoney and MoneyGuide Pro can factor inflation into long-term projections, but the concept is simple: $50,000 today won't buy as much 20 years from now.

Earlier in the book, we reviewed foundational income sources like Social Security and pensions. Depending on your personal strategy, you might also use annuities to generate income. In addition, you will also be likely to withdraw funds from your investment accounts. How you coordinate these sources can influence factors such as taxes and overall confidence in the plan.

Each of the retirement income approaches we've discussed, including Total Return, Income Protection (Flooring), Risk Wrap, and Time Segmentation (Bucket), offers a different method for generating monthly income. While these methods vary, most retirees share a common goal: creating a stable and predictable income stream that supports their lifestyle. Thinking in terms of monthly income often helps bring clarity and structure to the overall plan, especially since most people are accustomed to managing their finances around monthly expenses.

Once your plan is in place, many people review it reguarily. Life changes, markets fluctuate, and inflation can impact your spending power. A review gives you a chance to reassess how well the plan is working and whether adjustments are needed. For example, a sharp market downturn might affect a Total Return strategy more than a Flooring approach. The goal is to check whether the plan still aligns with your needs and risk tolerance, especially during volatile times.

It's also important to consider the timing and impact of required minimum distributions (RMDs). These mandatory withdrawals from certain retirement accounts can increase your taxable income, so it's important to plan. Many income planning approaches take this into account, along with asset location strategies, to help reduce tax drag and keep your money working efficiently.

Flexibility is also important. A rigid income plan can leave you vulnerable to surprise expenses or lifestyle changes. Just like your pre-retirement budget had some wiggle room, your retirement plan should too. Building in some flexibility helps you absorb unexpected costs without scrambling.

Technology can support this process, from simple budgeting tools to comprehensive retirement planning software. Even a well-structured spreadsheet can help keep things organized. What tends to matter most is that you understand how the pieces of your income plan fit together.

A few common pitfalls are worth mentioning. Failing to coordinate income sources across accounts can lead to unnecessary taxes or missed opportunities. Ignoring inflation or tax drag can erode your long-term sustainability. And sometimes the fear of running out of money leads retirees to underspend early on, potentially leaving lifestyle goals unfulfilled.

That fear is understandable. Retirement may last 30 years or more, and none of us can predict how long we'll live or what our needs will be down the road. But the goal is not to be perfect. It's to be prepared.

Reflection Questions

- Do you have a clear sense of how much income you'll need each month in retirement?
- How will inflation affect your spending needs over time?
- Which income sources will provide your retirement paycheck?
- How confident are you in your ability to coordinate withdrawals across accounts?
- What strategies or tools could help you stay on track year after year?

WHY THIS ISN'T SIMPLE

If you've made it through this chapter, you've probably realized something: creating a retirement income plan is not a matter of filling in a few blanks or checking off a short to-do list. This is not a plug-and-play formula. It involves coordinating multiple accounts, selecting an income strategy, adjusting for inflation, understanding taxes, planning for longevity, and dealing with the emotions that come from watching your savings turn into spending.

Even in a chapter focused on education, we've covered a lot: risk, return, income types, behavior, strategy alignment, and ongoing review. Retirement planning is a process, not an event. The decisions are interconnected and often complex, and they change over time.

You don't have to solve everything all at once. But it's worth recognizing that this stage of financial planning comes with new challenges and that those challenges deserve serious thought. Whether you manage this yourself or seek help, give your retirement paycheck the same attention you gave to building your savings. It's your turn to get paid.

References

1. Financial Perspectives. "Sequence of Returns Risk and Retirement." March 18, 2015. Available at: https://www.financialperspectives.biz/perspectives-retirement-blog/gc1i1jbbe90kg2rxggrpk7hugeva73

2. U.S. Bureau of Labor Statistics. "Consumer Price Index Data." Historical data accessed via FRED: https://fred.stlouisfed.org/series/CUUR0000SETA01

3. Social Security Administration. "Actuarial Life Table." Available at: https://www.ssa.gov/oact/STATS/table4c6.html

4. Pfau, Wade D., and Murguia, Alex. *RISA: A Framework for Matching Retirement Income Strategies to Client Preferences.* Published by Kitces.com. Available at: https://www.kitces.com/blog/risa-framework-retirement-income-planning-client-preferences-total-return-strategy-risk-tolerance/

5. Murguía, A., & Pfau, W. D. (2022). *RISA® Matrix Retirement Strategy Frequency Distributions.* Protected Income. Retrieved from https://www.protectedincome.org/wp-content/uploads/2022/11/RP-18B_Murguia_Pfau_Nov_v4.pdf

6. Society of Actuaries & LIMRA. (2023). *Fixed Indexed Annuity Contract Owner Behavior Study.* Retrieved from https://www.loma.org/en/news/press-releases/2023/new-study-examines-fixed-indexed-annuity-contract-owner-behavior/

CHAPTER 9
PROTECTING YOURSELF AND YOUR LEGACY

If you've made it this far, you've already built something worth protecting. You've taken steps toward building a retirement plan that considers income, investment strategies, taxes, and lifestyle. You've put in the hard work to get organized, think long-term, and take a more intentional approach to your future. This chapter turns to a part of the plan that many people delay - what happens if your health changes, and what happens after you're gone?

This chapter isn't about fear. It's about readiness.

Planning for long-term care and estate issues isn't a signal that something is wrong. It's a way of saying, "I care about the people around me. I've worked hard to build this, and I want to protect it." And yet, this is the part of financial planning that tends to get pushed off. People say, *We'll take care of that next year* or *after vacation* or *once things slow down*. But next year often turns into five years, and nothing gets done.

It's time to bring this conversation to the forefront.

If you've already taken care of this planning, that's great. But when was the last time you looked at it? Does your will still reflect your wishes? Is your executor still alive, capable, and willing to take on the responsibility? Are the people listed on your healthcare directive still the best choices? Have your assets changed, or your relationships?

This isn't just about legal documents. It's about keeping your financial life protected, and your loved ones supported through a wide range of possible outcomes.

In the pages that follow, we'll walk through:

- What long-term care really means, and how to evaluate your options
- The real costs of care and the risk of ignoring them
- What Medicaid does and doesn't cover (and why Medicare isn't a solution)
- The estate planning documents everyone needs, starting at age 18
- Common gaps and how to avoid them
- And a few next steps to make sure your plan stays up to date

Now that you've taken steps towards building a retirement plan, this chapter focuses on how those plans can be protected both during your lifetime and after.

This material does not provide legal advice. Please consult an attorney for guidance specific to your situation.

LONG-TERM CARE: PLANNING FOR THE UNEXPECTED

You may spend years budgeting, investing, and working toward a retirement plan. But have you thought about what happens if you or your spouse needs help getting through the day? Long-term care is one of the more commonly overlooked areas in retirement planning. Most people assume Medicare will cover it, or that it's something they won't need. In practice, coverag and need often look very different.

HOW LIKELY ARE YOU TO NEED CARE?

Roughly 70% of people turning 65 today will need some form of long-term care during their lives. That could mean a few months of in-home care, or several years in a nursing facility. On average, women need care longer than men, about 3.7 years versus 2.2 years, respectively [1].

Many people assume this kind of care only comes at the very end of life. But it can also follow a surgery, a chronic illness like Parkinson's or Alzheimer's, or even a long recovery after a fall. It's not always

144

permanent condition, but it is can be a financial stressor if you don't have a plan.

What Does Long-Term Care Cost?

Long-term care is expensive, and those costs are rising. As of 2024, national median monthly costs look like this [2]:

- Home health aide (44 hours/week): $6,500
- Assisted living facility: $5,900
- Nursing home (semi-private room): $9,277
- Nursing home (private room): $10,646

Keep in mind these are averages. In high-cost states or metro areas, costs can run much higher. And since care may be needed for several years, it's easy to see how this could total hundreds of thousands of dollars over time.

Can You Self-Fund?

Some people plan to cover long-term care costs using personal savings, investments, or home equity. This can work if you have significant resources, but it still typically involves careful planning.

Let's say you required three years of nursing home care in a private room. At today's average cost, that adds up to over $350,000. Add a few more years of in-home care before that, and the total could approach or exceed $500,000 [2]. For those considering self-funding, setting money aside early and revisiting the plan periodically can be part of the process.

Long-Term Care Insurance: What to Know

Long-term care insurance can help cover some of these costs. These policies typically pay a daily or monthly benefit for care services in your home or in a facility, once certain conditions are met.

When reviewing a policy, here are a few things to look for:

- Inflation protection: Without it, your benefit may fall behind the rising cost of care.

- Daily or monthly benefit: How much would the policy pay per day, and is that enough based on where you live?
- Type of care covered: Some older policies only cover nursing home care. Newer ones often include home care or assisted living.
- Waiting period: This is like a deductible. It's the number of days you'll pay out of pocket before benefits begin.

Premiums vary widely. For example, a healthy 60-year-old buying a policy with $165,000 in total coverage (indexed at 3% per year) might expect to pay between $2,610 and $4,550 annually [3]. It's not cheap, but some people value the additional predictability it can add, especially for couples or individuals with limited family support.

WHAT MEDICARE AND MEDICAID REALLY COVER

Medicare is not a long-term care plan. It may cover up to 100 days in a skilled nursing facility following a qualifying hospital stay of at least three days. However, full coverage only lasts for 20 days, and partial coverage continues for up to 80 more. Medicare does not pay for ongoing custodial care like assistance with bathing, dressing, or eating [4].

Medicaid can help pay for long-term care, but only for individuals who meet strict income and asset limits. In Wisconsin, a single applicant must have no more than $2,000 in countable assets to qualify for long-term care services. Married couples may have different limits depending on whether one or both spouses are applying. The non-applicant spouse may retain up to $157,920 in assets under the Community Spouse Resource Allowance [5].

To qualify, individuals often go through a "spend-down" process, using their assets to pay for care until they fall below Medicaid's financial thresholds. This can include spending on medical expenses, home modifications, or care services. It's important to keep documentation to show how funds were used, as Medicaid reviews eligibility closely [6].

ESTATE PLANNING: DON'T LEAVE IT TO CHANCE

If something unexpected happened tomorrow, would your family know what to do? Would they have the legal authority to act on your behalf? Would your assets go where you want them to go, or would the court decide?

Estate planning is often treated as something for the wealthy or the elderly. But in practice, it's something every adult should have in place. Once you're over 18, having basic estate planning documents becomes relevant, regardless of income or net worth. It doesn't matter how much you have in the bank or whether you own a home. This is about helping ensure the people you trust are legally able to step in if something happens, and making sure your wishes are clearly communicated.

This isn't about fear. It's about responsibility. Without an estate plan, your family could face confusion, court delays, or even legal battles during an already stressful time. But with a plan in place, you can create clarity and confidence for the people who care about you most.

THE CORE DOCUMENTS EVERYONE SHOULD HAVE

Here are the foundational pieces of an estate plan and what each one does:

- **Will**
  This document directs where your assets go after your death. It names an executor who will handle your estate and can also name guardians for minor children. Without a will, your state's intestacy laws decide what happens, and that may not match your wishes.
- **Durable Power of Attorney (POA)**
  This gives someone you trust the ability to make financial or legal decisions for you if you become incapacitated. Without it,

147

your family may have to go to court just to manage your accounts or pay your bills.

- **Healthcare Power of Attorney**
  This names someone to make medical decisions for you if you're unable to speak for yourself. It is designed to help ensure that your preferences are followed and that someone you trust is in charge.
- **Advance Directive (Living Will)**
  This document lets you express your wishes for end-of-life medical care. It guides your healthcare POA and your doctors so they know what treatments you do or do not want.
- **HIPAA Release**
  This allows your designated decision-makers to access your medical records. Without it, even your spouse or children may be blocked from getting important information.

WHAT ABOUT TRUSTS AND MORE ADVANCED PLANNING?

In addition to the core documents, some individuals and families may benefit from additional tools like:

- **Revocable Living Trusts**
  These allow your assets to be managed during your lifetime and transferred after death without going through probate. They can also help in situations where privacy, incapacity, or out-of-state property is involved.
- **Irrevocable Trusts**
  Often used for asset protection, charitable giving, or Medicaid planning. Once created, they cannot be changed easily, so they require careful legal guidance.
- **Special Needs Trusts**
  Designed to help provide for a disabled child or adult without jeopardizing government benefits. These require very specific legal language and are usually handles with specialized legal help.
- **Business Succession Plans**
  If you own a business, estate plans often address what happens to

it. Without a clear plan, operations can be disrupted or the business may be forced to liquidate.

- **Beneficiary Designations**
  Retirement accounts and life insurance policies pass directly to named beneficiaries. These need to be kept up to date and aligned with your overall estate plan.

COMMON GAPS THAT CAUSE REAL PROBLEMS

Even people who feel they have a solid plan can run into trouble if they overlook a few key details. Here are some of the most common gaps:

- Outdated beneficiary designations on IRAs, 401(k)s, or life insurance
- Accounts or property not titled properly, causing them to bypass the will or trust
- No plan for digital assets like email, cloud storage, or cryptocurrency
- No backup agents listed in power of attorney documents
- Not discussing the plan with heirs, beneficiaries, or even a spouse
- Relying on outdated templates or online forms that may not reflect current laws or personal circumstances

Checklist: Estate Planning Gaps to Avoid

- Are your beneficiaries up to date across all accounts?
- Is your will signed and current?
- Do you have both financial and healthcare powers of attorney?
- Are your digital assets accessible with clear instructions?
- Have you reviewed your plan in the past 3 to 5 years?
- Have you talked to your spouse, children, or executor about your wishes?

A Note on Legal Help

Estate planning is not well suited to a do-it-yourself project. While basic documents are available online, estate laws vary by state and small mistakes can create big problems later. For that reason, these documents should be prepared or reviewed by an attorney who understands both your state's laws and your personal situation.

This isn't about hiring a team of experts or spending a fortune. It's about putting the right documents in place, informing the right people, and clearly documenting your wishes.

BEFORE YOU CLOSE THIS CHAPTER: MAKE SURE SOMEONE ELSE KNOWS THE PLAN

In many households, one person handles most of the financial decisions. It might be the spouse who pays the bills, manages the investments, or keeps track of the insurance policies. And while that can work well while both spouses are healthy, it can cause serious challenges if the one "in the know" is suddenly no longer there.

I've seen this happen too often. A spouse passes away unexpectedly, and the survivor is left confused and scared. They may not know where the accounts are held, who to contact, or even what insurance policies exist. In some cases, the children are just as lost. It's like being dropped into a crisis without a map, and it tends to lead to stress, delay, and painful mistakes.

If you are the person who manages the family's finances, you have a responsibility to make sure others can step in if needed. That doesn't mean giving up control. It means helping ensure your spouse, or someone you trust, knows how to take over if something happens to you.

Here's a simple step you can take: create a written reference. This could be a folder, a spreadsheet, or even a letter, stored securely in your home or with your estate documents. Include key information like:
- Contact info for your financial advisor, accountant, and attorney
- Life insurance and long-term care policy details
- Account numbers and financial institution names
- Password storage or access instructions (if applicable)
- Where to find your estate plan documents

- Any key instructions or preferences not already written into legal documents

This doesn't have to be perfect. It just needs to exist, and it benefits from being updated regularly. You don't want your spouse or children trying to guess what you would have wanted in the middle of an already difficult time.

A good estate plan isn't just about what happens after you're gone. It's about making life easier for the people you care about. Don't leave them in the dark. Write it down, talk it through, and make sure someone else knows the plan.

References

1. U.S. Department of Health and Human Services, Administration for Community Living. *How Much Care Will You Need?* https://acl.gov/ltc/basic-needs/how-much-care-will-you-need

2. Genworth Financial. *Cost of Care Survey 2024.* https://www.genworth.com/aging-and-you/finances/cost-of-care.html

3. American Association for Long-Term Care Insurance. *2025 Long-Term Care Insurance Statistics — Annual Premiums by Age and Benefit Level.* Jan 2025. (Table: purchase age 60, $165,000 benefit, 3% inflation growth option — single male $2,610; single female $4,550). https://www.aaltci.org/long-term-care-insurance/learning-center/ltcfacts-2025.php

4. Medicare.gov. *Skilled Nursing Facility (SNF) Care.* https://www.medicare.gov/coverage/skilled-nursing-facility-snf-care

5. Medicaid Planning Assistance. *Wisconsin Medicaid Long Term Care Programs.* https://www.medicaidlongtermcare.org/eligibility/wisconsin/

6. National Council on Aging. *What Is a Medicaid Spend Down?* https://www.ncoa.org/article/what-is-medicaid-spend-down/

CHAPTER 10
THE ONGOING PROCESS: ADAPTING YOUR PLAN

By now, you've seen how retirement planning is approached from an advisor's perspective: deliberate, informed, and customized to your life. You've explored strategies for saving, investing, managing taxes, generating income, and protecting your legacy. But even the best-designed plan is not the final word.

Thinking like an advisor means recognizing that planning is not a one-time event. It is an ongoing process. The strategies you put in place today are designed to adapt as life unfolds, markets move, and your goals evolve. This final chapter is about keeping your plan active and current, focused on keeping your plan active and current, so it stays aligned with where you are now and where you want to go.

Retirement planning does not stop when you retire. If anything, that is when the real work begins. The market will shift, tax laws will evolve, and your personal goals and expenses will change over time. A retirement plan that works at 65 may not be the right plan at 75 or 85.

This is why retirement plans are revisited over time. They are not built on the assumption that a good strategy today will stay that way forever. Conditions change, priorities evolve, and plans need to adapt. Many retirees who feel confident about their plans tend to follow a similar mindset. Rather than reacting impulsively to change, they focus on adjusting their plan.

Thinking like an advisor means staying engaged and being willing to course-correct when needed. A retirement plan is not a set of documents you file away. It is a living, breathing process.

WHY RETIREMENT IS NOT A ONE-TIME EVENT

One common misconception about retirement is that once you've created a plan, you are done. In reality, the retirement phase introduces its own set of variables that deserve attention. A single unexpected event can ripple across your income plan, tax outlook, and lifestyle.

Markets may drop sharply. Required minimum distributions can push you into a higher tax bracket. A health scare might change your spending needs overnight. Inflation quietly chips away at your purchasing power. Even changes in your family, such as grandchildren, a spouse's illness, or relocating, can shift your priorities.

Retirement is not a finish line. It is a new chapter, and like every good story, the plot will keep developing. Your plan is expected to evolve with along with it.

REGULAR REVIEWS, NOT CONSTANT CHANGES

Thinking like a financial advisor does not mean reworking your plan every year. It means checking in regularly and making changes only when they are appropriate.

If you are in your 40s and steadily saving for retirement, your plan might not call for much tinkering from year to year. You may be focused on maximizing contributions, managing debt, or raising children. A quick review to confirm you are still on track may be sufficient.

But if you are in your 60s and preparing to retire in the next few years, your plan likely requires more attention. You may want to revisit your withdrawal strategy, healthcare coverage, or Social Security timing. And once you are in retirement, spending patterns, taxes, and investment risks should be reviewed more frequently.

The key is not how often you make changes, it is how often you pay attention. Many advisors suggest reviewing your plan at least once a year, but not every review will result in action. Sometimes the outcome of a good review is simply confirmation that you are still on track.

WHAT AN ADVISOR LOOKS AT DURING A REVIEW

Reviews are not only conducted when problems arise. Regular check-ins can help identify small issues before they grow more complex. Adopting an advisor-style mindset often begins with building a habit of reviewing your plan on a regular basis.

ASSET ALLOCATION AND PORTFOLIO DRIFT

Even if you never make a single trade, your portfolio changes. Some investments grow faster than others, and over time, your original mix of stocks, bonds, and other assets drifts out of alignment. This is called portfolio drift.

For example, suppose you started with 60 percent stocks and 40 percent bonds. After a strong market run, that could shift to 70 percent stocks and only 30 percent bonds. This can result in taking on more risk than originally intended.

This is why automatic rebalancing is commonly used. These systems are designed to review and reset portfolios periodically, often once or twice a year, without emotional interference. This reduces the temptation to time the market or guess the best moment to make a move.

Whether automated or manual, rebalancing helps maintain your risk level and ensures your portfolio stays aligned with your goals.

WITHDRAWAL STRATEGY AND TAX PLANNING

Where you pull your money from can have a major impact on your tax bill. The wrong order of withdrawals can lead to paying more taxes than necessary. A commonly discussed framework is to start with taxable brokerage accounts, then moving to traditional tax-deferred accounts, and using Roth accounts last. But this is not a fixed rule.

In some years, it might make sense to do Roth conversions to shift money into tax-free accounts before you hit required minimum distributions. In other years, you may want to use Qualified Charitable

Distributions to lower your taxable income. Even the timing of a large expense can affect which account is best to draw from.

As taxes and income needs change, strategies often evolve as well.

SPENDING REVIEW

Your retirement spending plan is not static. While some costs remain steady, others can creep up. Subscriptions, travel, insurance premiums, or support for family members can all shift over time.

It is helpful to compare actual spending to your original projections. If you are consistently over budget, it might be time to reassess your withdrawal rate. If you are under budget, that could be an opportunity to enjoy your money more or gift intentionally.

This type of review can also prompt consideration of new goals. Maybe you want to take a special trip next year or help a grandchild with college. Ideally, your plan reflects your current priorities, not just what you wrote down five years ago.

HEALTHCARE AND INSURANCE NEEDS

Healthcare is one of the most dynamic expenses in retirement. Plans change, costs rise, and your personal medical needs may evolve quickly.

It can be useful to review Medicare coverage to see if it still fits. Prescription costs, network coverage, and plan premiums can shift from year to year. If you have a supplemental policy or long-term care coverage, review the benefits and confirm whether inflation protection is included.

It is also a good time to consider whether you need to add or drop coverage. Are you overinsured for something that no longer applies? Are you underinsured for a new risk?

ESTATE PLANNING AND TRUST UPDATES

Estate planning is not just about having documents. It is about keeping them relevant. Every few years or after major life events, you should review the key parts of your plan.

Wills and beneficiary designations should be kept up to date. So should trusts. Many people assume that once a trust is created, it never needs to be changed. In practice, that is often not the case. Laws governing trusts can evolve, and your family situation might shift. The trust you created 15 years ago may not reflect your current wishes or the most tax-efficient structure.

If you have a revocable living trust, it should be reviewed to ensure it still matches your estate strategy. If you have an irrevocable trust, it may require special attention to ensure compliance with current laws and planning goals.

A qualified estate attorney can help assess whether changes are warranted. Trusts are powerful tools, but only when they are current and properly aligned with your overall plan.

PERSONAL GOALS AND WHAT'S NEXT

Retirement is not just about preserving assets. It is about enjoying them. As your circumstances and interests change, your financial plan should support those changes.

Ask yourself what you want the next year to look like. Do you want to travel more? Volunteer? Start a business? Reduce responsibilities and simplify your life?

Your financial plan is a tool. It's worth checking whether it is still supporting the life you want.

PLANNING FOR WHAT YOU CANNOT PREDICT

Even with regular reviews, some things will happen that are outside your control. Markets will go through unexpected downturns. Health events may arrive without warning. Family dynamics can change in an instant.

This is why flexibility is often an important part of a retirement plan. That might mean maintaining a cash buffer to help avoid selling investments during a market downturn. It could involve identifying which expenses are essential versus discretionary, making adjustments easier in tougher years. It might also include stress-testing the plan against different scenarios, such as a bear market or an earlier-than-expected need for care.

You do not have to predict the future. What matters is having a structure that allows you to respond to it.

THE MINDSET THAT HELPS KEEP YOU ON TRACK

What ultimately helps keep people on track is not the ability to predict the future, but the willingness to expect change and build systems that can adapt. Plans are revisited. Better questions are asked. Learning continues as life unfolds.

If you've read this far, you've been exposed to much of that mindset. The theme throughout this book is that success in retirement is not driven by one-time decisions. It comes from consistent habits and thoughtful adjustments over time.

You don't need a perfect plan. What matters more is having a process. One that is reviewed regularly, refined as circumstances change, and grounded in curiosity rather than fear. The goal is not simply to make your money last, but to support the life you want to live.

You've built something worth protecting. Stay flexible. Keep paying attention. And continue thinking deliberately about the choices that shape your financial future.

CONCLUSION: KEEP THINKING LIKE AN ADVISOR

You made it. You've worked your way through many of the core concepts in retirement planning, including cash flow, investment strategies, taxes, income planning, healthcare, and legacy. More importantly, the book emphasized how to approach each topic with a clear, steady mindset.

This book was not about turning you into a financial advisor. It was about helping you think like one. Most advisors do not have all the answers; instead, they follow a process. They stay informed, revisit plans, and focus on long-term outcomes. The same process-oriented approach is accessible to individuals as well.

Whether you plan to manage everything yourself or eventually work with a professional, you are now better positioned to make thoughtful and confident decisions about your retirement. Throughout the book, financial planning has been framed as something that unfolds over time, not a one-time event. It is a series of informed choices made over time, based on your goals and values.

So what comes next?

Keeping your plan alive involves reviewing it periodically, talking with your spouse or family members, writing down what matters to you, asking questions when something changes, and staying involved.

You may also find that after working through all of these concepts, there is more to retirement planning than you originally thought. That is not a failure. It is clarity. At some point, it might make sense to seek a second opinion from a trusted advisor. Not because you cannot do it yourself, but because a second opinion can reveal things you might miss. An outside perspective can be especially valuable when decisions become more complex or the stakes feel higher. Many advisors offer this type of review for a flat fee or hourly rate, without requiring an ongoing relationship. It is simply another tool to help you move forward with confidence.

Above all, stay calm and focused. When others are reacting to the headlines, a clear process can help guide your decisions. This approach emphasizes preparation over prediction and discipline over reaction. It is designed to support thoughtful choices over time.

APPENDIX A: CALLAN CHART

The Callan Periodic Table of Investment Returns

Annual Returns for Key Indices Ranked in Order of Performance (2005–2024)

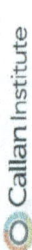

2005	2006	2007	2008	2009	2010	2011	2012	2013	2014
Emerging Market Equity 34.00%	Real Estate 42.12%	Emerging Market Equity 39.38%	U.S. Fixed Income 5.24%	Emerging Market Equity 78.51%	Small Cap Equity 26.85%	U.S. Fixed Income 7.84%	Real Estate 27.73%	Small Cap Equity 38.82%	Real Estate 15.02%
Real Estate 15.35%	Emerging Market Equity 32.17%	Developed ex-U.S. Equity 12.44%	Global ex-U.S. Fixed 4.39%	High Yield 58.21%	Real Estate 19.63%	High Yield 4.98%	Emerging Market Equity 18.23%	Large Cap Equity 32.39%	Large Cap Equity 13.69%
Developed ex-U.S. Equity 14.47%	Developed ex-U.S. Equity 25.71%	Global ex-U.S. Fixed 11.03%	Cash Equivalent 2.06%	Real Estate 37.13%	Emerging Market Equity 18.88%	Global ex-U.S. Fixed 4.36%	Developed ex-U.S. Equity 16.41%	Developed ex-U.S. Equity 21.02%	U.S. Fixed Income 5.97%
Large Cap Equity 4.91%	Small Cap Equity 18.37%	U.S. Fixed Income 6.97%	High Yield -26.16%	Developed ex-U.S. Equity 33.67%	High Yield 15.12%	Large Cap Equity 2.11%	Small Cap Equity 16.35%	High Yield 7.44%	Small Cap Equity 4.89%
Small Cap Equity 4.55%	Large Cap Equity 15.79%	Large Cap Equity 5.49%	Small Cap Equity -33.79%	Small Cap Equity 27.17%	Large Cap Equity 15.06%	Cash Equivalent 0.10%	Large Cap Equity 16.00%	Real Estate 3.67%	High Yield 2.45%
Cash Equivalent 3.07%	High Yield 11.85%	Cash Equivalent 5.00%	Large Cap Equity -37.00%	Large Cap Equity 26.47%	Developed ex-U.S. Equity 8.95%	Small Cap Equity -4.18%	High Yield 15.81%	Cash Equivalent 0.07%	Cash Equivalent 0.03%
High Yield 2.74%	Global ex-U.S. Fixed 8.16%	High Yield 1.87%	Developed ex-U.S. Equity -43.56%	Global ex-U.S. Fixed 7.53%	U.S. Fixed Income 6.54%	Real Estate -6.46%	U.S. Fixed Income 4.21%	U.S. Fixed Income -2.02%	Emerging Market Equity -2.19%
U.S. Fixed Income 2.43%	Cash Equivalent 4.85%	Small Cap Equity -1.57%	Real Estate -48.21%	U.S. Fixed Income 5.93%	Global ex-U.S. Fixed 4.95%	Developed ex-U.S. Equity -12.21%	Global ex-U.S. Fixed 4.09%	Emerging Market Equity -2.60%	Global ex-U.S. Fixed -3.09%
Global ex-U.S. Fixed -8.65%	U.S. Fixed Income 4.33%	Real Estate -7.39%	Emerging Market Equity -53.33%	Cash Equivalent 0.21%	Cash Equivalent 0.13%	Emerging Market Equity -18.42%	Cash Equivalent 0.11%	Global ex-U.S. Fixed -3.08%	Developed ex-U.S. Equity -4.32%

2015	2016	2017	2018	2019	2020	2021	2022	2023	2024
Large Cap Equity 1.38%	Small Cap Equity 21.31%	Emerging Market Equity 37.28%	Cash Equivalent 1.87%	Large Cap Equity 31.49%	Small Cap Equity 19.96%	Large Cap Equity 28.71%	Cash Equivalent 1.46%	Large Cap Equity 26.29%	Large Cap Equity 25.02%
U.S. Fixed Income 0.55%	High Yield 17.13%	Developed ex-U.S. Equity 24.21%	U.S. Fixed Income 0.01%	Small Cap Equity 25.52%	Large Cap Equity 18.40%	Real Estate 26.09%	High Yield -11.19%	Developed ex-U.S. Equity 17.94%	Small Cap Equity 11.54%
Cash Equivalent 0.05%	Large Cap Equity 11.96%	Large Cap Equity 21.83%	High Yield -2.08%	Developed ex-U.S. Equity 22.49%	Emerging Market Equity 18.31%	Small Cap Equity 14.82%	U.S. Fixed Income -13.01%	Small Cap Equity 16.93%	High Yield 8.19%
Real Estate -0.79%	Emerging Market Equity 11.19%	Small Cap Equity 14.65%	Global ex-U.S. Fixed -2.15%	Real Estate 21.91%	Global ex-U.S. Fixed 10.11%	Developed ex-U.S. Equity 12.62%	Developed ex-U.S. Equity -14.29%	High Yield 13.44%	Emerging Market Equity 7.50%
Developed ex-U.S. Equity -3.04%	Real Estate 4.06%	Global ex-U.S. Fixed 10.51%	Large Cap Equity -4.38%	Emerging Market Equity 18.44%	Developed ex-U.S. Equity 7.59%	High Yield 5.28%	Large Cap Equity -18.11%	Emerging Market Equity 9.83%	Cash Equivalent 5.25%
Small Cap Equity -4.41%	Developed ex-U.S. Equity 2.75%	Real Estate 10.36%	Real Estate -5.63%	High Yield 14.32%	U.S. Fixed Income 7.51%	Cash Equivalent 0.05%	Global ex-U.S. Fixed -18.70%	Real Estate 9.67%	Developed ex-U.S. Equity 4.70%
High Yield -4.47%	U.S. Fixed Income 2.65%	High Yield 7.50%	Small Cap Equity -11.01%	U.S. Fixed Income 8.72%	High Yield 7.11%	U.S. Fixed Income -1.54%	Emerging Market Equity -20.09%	Global ex-U.S. Fixed 5.72%	U.S. Fixed Income 1.25%
Global ex-U.S. Fixed -6.02%	Global ex-U.S. Fixed 1.49%	U.S. Fixed Income 3.54%	Developed ex-U.S. Equity -14.09%	Global ex-U.S. Fixed 5.09%	Cash Equivalent 0.67%	Emerging Market Equity -2.54%	Small Cap Equity -20.44%	U.S. Fixed Income 5.53%	Real Estate 0.94%
Emerging Market Equity -14.92%	Cash Equivalent 0.33%	Cash Equivalent 0.86%	Emerging Market Equity -14.57%	Cash Equivalent 2.28%	Real Estate -9.04%	Global ex-U.S. Fixed -7.05%	Real Estate -25.10%	Cash Equivalent 5.01%	Global ex-U.S. Fixed -4.22%

The Callan Periodic Table of Investment Returns conveys the strong ***case for diversification*** across asset classes (stocks vs. bonds), capitalizations (large vs. small), and equity markets (U.S. vs. global ex-U.S.). The Table highlights the uncertainty inherent in all capital markets. Rankings change every year. Also noteworthy is the difference between absolute and relative performance, as returns for the top-performing asset class span a wide range over the past 20 years.

A printable copy of The Callan Periodic Table of Investment Returns is available on our website at ***callan.com/periodic-table/***

Callan Institute

Research | Education | Dialogue

The Callan Periodic Table of Investment Returns 2005–2024

Callan's Periodic Table of Investment Returns depicts annual returns for 8 asset classes and cash equivalents, ranked from best to worst performance for each calendar year. The asset classes are color-coded to enable easy tracking over time. We describe the well-known, industry-standard market indices that we use as proxies for each asset class below.

- **Large Cap Equity (S&P 500)** measures the performance of large capitalization U.S. stocks. The S&P 500 is a market-value-weighted index of 500 stocks. The weightings make each company's influence on the Index performance directly proportional to that company's market value.

- **Small Cap Equity (Russell 2000)** measures the performance of small capitalization U.S. stocks. The Russell 2000 is a market-value-weighted index of the 2,000 smallest stocks in the broad-market Russell 3000 Index.

- **Developed ex-U.S. Equity (MSCI World ex USA)** is an index that is designed to measure the performance of large and mid cap equities in developed markets in Europe, the Middle East, the Pacific region, and Canada.

- **Emerging Market Equity (MSCI Emerging Markets)** is an index that is designed to measure the performance of equity markets in 24 emerging countries around the world.

- **U.S. Fixed Income (Bloomberg US Aggregate Bond Index)** includes U.S. government, corporate, and mortgage-backed securities with maturities of at least one year.

- **High Yield (Bloomberg High Yield Bond Index)** measures the market of USD-denominated, non-investment grade, fixed-rate, taxable corporate bonds. Securities are classified as high yield if the middle rating of Moody's, Fitch, and S&P is Ba1/BB+/BB+ or below, excluding emerging market debt.

- **Global ex-U.S. Fixed Income (Bloomberg Global Aggregate ex US Bond Index)** is an unmanaged index that is comprised of several other Bloomberg indices that measure the fixed income performance of regions around the world, excluding the U.S.

- **Real Estate (FTSE EPRA Nareit Developed REIT Index)** is designed to measure the stock performance of companies engaged in specific real estate activities in the North American, European, and Asian real estate markets.

- **Cash Equivalent (90-day T-bill)** is a short-term debt obligation backed by the Treasury Department of the U.S. government.

Callan

Callan was founded as an employee-owned investment consulting firm in 1973. Ever since, we have empowered institutional investor clients with creative, customized investment solutions backed by proprietary research, exclusive data, and ongoing education. Today, Callan provides advisory services to institutional investor clients with more than $3 trillion in total assets, which makes it among the largest independently owned investment consulting firms in the U.S. Callan uses a client-focused consulting model to serve pension and defined contribution plan sponsors, endowments, foundations, independent investment advisers, investment managers, and other asset owners. Callan has six offices throughout the U.S. Learn more at callan.com.

Corporate Headquarters: San Francisco

Regional Consulting Offices: Atlanta, Chicago, Denver, Portland, and Summit, NJ

APPENDIX B: A READER CHECKLIST

Big Picture

☐ I understand that retirement planning is not a one-time decision

☐ I can explain my financial strategy in plain language

☐ I know what my money is meant to support, not just how it is invested

Financial Foundation

☐ I know where all my accounts are and what they are for

☐ I have an emergency fund separate from investments

☐ I understand how my debt affects future cash flow

☐ My insurance coverage reflects my current life stage

Saving Strategy

☐ I am saving consistently and intentionally

☐ I know my approximate savings rate

☐ I use more than one type of account (traditional, Roth, taxable)

☐ I understand the tradeoffs between tax-deferred and tax-free savings

Investing Mindset

☐ I have a written investment rationale or process

☐ I understand my portfolio's risk and diversification

☐ I know where different investments are held and why

☐ I am aware of investment costs and what I'm paying for

Income Awareness

☐ I know my likely income sources in retirement

☐ I understand which income is guaranteed and which is variable

☐ I know how taxes affect different income streams

☐ I have thought about how income changes over time

Risk & Uncertainty

☐ I have considered healthcare and long-term care risks

☐ I know where flexibility exists in my plan

☐ I understand that uncertainty is normal, not a failure

☐ I revisit decisions instead of reacting emotionally

Ongoing Process

☐ I review my plan periodically, not constantly

☐ I adjust when circumstances change, not when headlines change

☐ I ask better questions than I used to

☐ I remain actively engaged in my financial life

The goal is not control.
The goal is clarity.
The goal is not prediction.
The goal is preparation.

APPENDIX C: KEY DEFINITIONS

RETIREMENT ACCOUNTS

Traditional IRA
A retirement account where your contributions may be tax-deductible today, but you pay taxes on the money when you withdraw it in retirement.

Roth IRA
A retirement account where you pay taxes on contributions now, but your money grows tax-free and withdrawals in retirement are tax-free.

401(k)
A workplace retirement plan where you save money directly from your paycheck, often with help from an employer match.

403(b)
A retirement plan similar to a 401(k), offered by schools, hospitals, and nonprofit organizations.

457(b)
A retirement plan for government and certain nonprofit employees that allows penalty-free withdrawals if you leave the job.

SEP IRA
A retirement account for self-employed people or small business owners with higher contribution limits.

SIMPLE IRA
A retirement plan for small businesses that includes required employer contributions and is easier to run than a 401(k).

Inherited IRA
An IRA you receive after someone dies, which has special rules for withdrawals.

Required Minimum Distribution (RMD)
The minimum amount you must withdraw each year from traditional retirement accounts beginning at age 73.

Backdoor Roth IRA
A method for high-income earners to fund a Roth IRA by contributing to a Traditional IRA and converting it.

Roth Conversion
Moving money from a traditional account to a Roth IRA and paying taxes now in exchange for tax-free growth later.

Qualified Charitable Distribution (QCD)
A donation made directly from an IRA to a charity that counts toward your RMD and is excluded from taxable income.

TAX CONCEPTS

Capital Gains
The profit you earn when selling an investment for more than you paid.

Ordinary Income
Income taxed at your regular income tax rates, including wages, interest, and most retirement withdrawals.

Marginal Tax Rate
The tax rate you pay on your next dollar of income.

Effective Tax Rate
Your average tax rate based on total taxes paid divided by total income.

Tax-Deferred Growth
Money that grows without being taxed until you withdraw it.

Tax-Free Growth
Money that grows and can be withdrawn completely tax-free.

Taxable Account
An investment account where interest, dividends, and capital gains may be taxed each year.

Cost Basis
The amount you originally paid for an investment, used to calculate taxes when you sell.

Step-Up in Basis
The reset of an investment's cost basis to its value at the owner's death.

Tax Loss Harvesting
Selling investments at a loss to offset taxable gains from other investments.

Provisional Income
The income formula used to determine how much of your Social Security benefit is taxable.

IRMAA
An extra Medicare premium charged to higher-income retirees.

INVESTMENT TERMS

Stocks
Shares of ownership in a company that can rise or fall in value.

Bonds
Loans you give to a company or government in exchange for interest payments.

Mutual Fund
A fund that pools money from many investors to buy a mix of investments.

ETF (Exchange Traded Fund)
A fund that trades like a stock and holds a basket of investments.

Index Fund
A low-cost fund that tracks a market benchmark, such as the S&P 500.

Actively Managed Fund
A fund where managers choose investments in an effort to beat the market.

Asset Allocation
How you divide your investments among stocks, bonds, and other assets.

Asset Location
Placing investments in accounts where they are most tax-efficient.

Diversification
Owning a mix of investments so one downturn does not hurt your entire portfolio.

Rebalancing
Adjusting investments to return to your target mix of stocks and bonds.

Total Return
The combined growth from investment gains, interest, and dividends.

Dividend Yield
The income a stock pays compared to its price.

Sequence of Returns Risk
The risk of experiencing bad market returns early in retirement when taking withdrawals.

Alternative Investments
Investments outside stocks and bonds, such as real estate or commodities.

Liquidity Risk
The risk of not being able to access your money when needed.

RETIREMENT INCOME PLANNING

Safe Withdrawal Rate
An estimate of how much you can withdraw each year without running out of money.

Guaranteed Income
Income that continues no matter how long you live, such as Social Security or certain annuities.

Longevity Risk
The risk of outliving your savings.

Inflation Risk
The risk that rising prices reduce your purchasing power.

Bridge Strategy
Using savings to delay Social Security for a higher benefit later.

Withdrawal Order
The sequence in which you draw from taxable, traditional, and Roth accounts.

Social Security

Primary Insurance Amount (PIA)
The amount you receive from Social Security at your full retirement age.

Full Retirement Age (FRA)
The age when you receive your full Social Security benefit, usually between 66 and 67.

Delayed Retirement Credits
Extra benefits earned for delaying Social Security past your FRA, up to age 70.

Spousal Benefits
Benefits that allow a spouse to receive up to 50 percent of their partner's FRA benefit.

Survivor Benefits
Payments available to a spouse when the higher-earning partner passes away.

Earnings Test
A rule that reduces your benefits if you claim early while still earning above certain limits.

FINANCIAL PLANNING TOOLS

Net Worth Statement
A list of everything you own and owe.

Cash Flow Statement
A summary of your income and expenses.

Emergency Fund
Money set aside for unexpected expenses.

Debt-to-Income Ratio
A measure of how much of your income goes to debt payments.

Compound Interest
Interest earned on both your original money and past interest.

Dollar-Cost Averaging
Investing the same amount regularly no matter the market conditions.

Monte Carlo Simulation
A tool that tests thousands of retirement scenarios to see how long your money may last.

ESTATE PLANNING

Will
A legal document stating who receives your assets after you die.

Revocable Living Trust
A tool that holds your assets and helps avoid probate.

Power of Attorney
A document allowing someone to make decisions for you if you cannot.

Healthcare Directive
Instructions for medical care if you cannot speak for yourself.

HIPAA Authorization
Permission to share your medical information with specific people.

Beneficiary Designation
The person who receives your retirement accounts or life insurance.

Probate
The court process that oversees distributing your assets.

RISA CONCEPTS

RISA
A tool that identifies how you prefer to build retirement income.

Bucket Strategy
A method of organizing your savings into short-term, mid-term, and long-term buckets to manage withdrawals.

Total Return Strategy
Using your entire investment portfolio to generate retirement income.

Income Floor
The minimum amount of income you know you can count on each month.

Risk Wrap
Using insurance features to add protection to market-based investments while still allowing for growth.

INSURANCE & RISK MANAGEMENT

Term Life Insurance
Coverage that lasts for a set period and pays a benefit if you die during that time.

Whole Life Insurance
Permanent insurance that lasts for your life and builds cash value.

1035 Exchange
A tax-free way to move cash value from one insurance policy to another.

Disability Insurance
Insurance that replaces part of your income if you cannot work.

Long-Term Care Insurance
Insurance that helps pay for nursing home care, assisted living, or in-home care.

Umbrella Insurance
Extra liability coverage beyond your home or auto policy.

Deductible
The amount you pay out of pocket before insurance coverage begins.

IMPORTANT DISCLOSURES

The information provided in this material is for educational purposes only and is not intended as investment, tax, or legal advice. Examples and illustrations are hypothetical and for informational purposes only; they do not represent actual results and are not guarantees of future performance.

Investing involves risk, including the possible loss of principal. Past performance is not indicative of future results. There is no assurance that any investment strategy will be successful.

Market conditions, interest rates, and other factors can change over time and may affect outcomes.

Tax and legal considerations vary by individual circumstances. You should consult with a qualified tax advisor, attorney, or financial professional before making decisions related to your personal situation.

References to third-party companies, products, or services (e.g. SSA.gov, Kiplinger, Investopedia) are provided for informational purposes only and do not constitute endorsement or recommendation. We are not affiliated with these organizations.

This material does not constitute an offer to buy or sell any security or investment product. All investments should be made based on your objectives, risk tolerance, and financial situation.

Converting from a traditional IRA to a Roth IRA is a taxable event.

The cost and availability of life insurance depend on factors such as age, health, and the type and amount of insurance purchased.

Before implementing a strategy involving life insurance, it would be prudent to make sure that you are insurable by having the policy approved. As with most financial decisions, there are expenses associated with the purchase of life insurance. Policies commonly have mortality and expense charges. In addition, if a policy is surrendered prematurely, there may be surrender charges and income tax implications.

www.ingramcontent.com/pod-product-compliance
Lightning Source LLC
Chambersburg PA
CBHW070421290526
45791CB00005B/1785